TOP **10**
CUBA

CHRISTOPHER P BAKER

EYEWITNESS TRAVEL

Left **The shoreline at Guardalacava** Right **View of Cordillera De Guaniguanico**

LONDON, NEW YORK,
MELBOURNE, MUNICH AND DELHI
www.dk.com

Design, Editorial, and Picture Research, by Quadrum Solutions,
Krishnamai, 33B, Sir Pochkanwala Road, Worli, Mumbai, India

Reproduced by Colourscan, Singapore
Printed and bound in China
by Leo Paper Products Ltd

First American Edition, 2008
10 11 12 13 10 9 8 7 6 5 4 3 2 1

Published in the United States by
DK Publishing, 375 Hudson Street, New York, New York
10014

Copyright 2008, 2010
© Dorling Kindersley Limited, London
A Penguin Company

Reprinted with revisions 2010

Published in Great Britain by Dorling Kindersley Limited.

A CIP catalogue record is available from the British Library.

ISSN 1479-344X
ISBN 978 0 7566 6174 8

Within each Top 10 list in this book, no hierarchy of quality
or popularity is implied. All 10 are, in the editor's opinion,
of roughly equal merit.

Floors are referred to throughout in accordance with British
usage; ie the "first floor" is the floor above ground level.

MIX
Paper from
responsible sources
FSC™ C018179
www.fsc.org

Contents

Cuba's Top 10

The information in this DK Eyewitness Top 10 Travel Guide is checked regularly.
Every effort has been made to ensure that this book is as up-to-date as possible at the time of
going to press. Some details, however, such as telephone numbers, opening hours, prices,
gallery hanging arrangements and travel information are liable to change. The publishers
cannot accept responsibility for any consequences arising from the use of this book, nor for
any material on third party websites, and cannot guarantee that any website address in this
book will be a suitable source of travel information. We value the views and suggestions of
our readers very highly. Please write to: Publisher, DK Eyewitness Travel Guides,
Dorling Kindersley, 80 Strand, London WC2R 0RL, Great Britain.

Cover: Front – **Hemispheres Images**: Herve Hughes bl; **Pictures Colour Library**: Clive Sawyer main.
Spine – **DK Images**: Heidi Grassley b. Back – **4Comers Images**: Ripani Massimo tr; **DK Images**: Heidi
Grassley tc; **Hemispheres Images**: Herve Hughes tl.

Left **Graffitied wall in Havana** Center **Turtle** Right **Musicians in Santiago de Cuba**

Contents

Left **Salón de los Pasos Perdidos, Capitolio** Right **Gran Car taxi in front of Hotel Nacional**

Key to abbreviations
Adm *admission charge* **Dis. access** *disabled access*

3

CUBA'S
TOP 10

CUBA'S TOP 10

🔟 Cuba Highlights

Cuba, the Caribbean's largest island, is a land of extraordinary beauty and amazing contrasts. From white-sand beaches and teal-blue seas to lush valleys and cloud-draped mountains, Cuba is kaleidoscopic in its terrains. Steeped in history, this Communist nation is in a time warp and brims with colonial buildings, pre-revolutionary 1950s cars, and rural villages. The country's vivacious populace is a blend of Spanish, African, and indigenous peoples.

① Habana Vieja, Havana
Colonial castles, palaces, and cobbled plazas make Old Havana the jewel in the crown of the capital city, recalling days when it was the New World's wealthiest city *(see pp8–9)*.

② The Modern City, Havana
This throbbing 20th-century metropolis encompasses interesting museums, spacious green parks, lovely white beaches, 1950s-era hotels and nightclubs, and stunning examples of latter-day architecture from Beaux Arts to *modernismo* *(see pp10–11)*.

③ Cordillera de Guaniguanico
A few hours west of Havana, these rugged mountains are a birder's and hiker's delight. The dramatic limestone formations rising over tobacco fields add surreal beauty to Valle de Viñales *(see pp12–13)*.

④ Zapata Peninsula
This vast swampland and park protects many of Cuba's crocodiles and endemic bird species *(left)*. It has great fishing flats and cave dive sites. Two museums recall the 1962 Bay of Pigs invasion *(see pp14–15)*.

⑤ Trinidad
Trinidad boasts a breeze-swept hillside setting. This UNESCO World Heritage Site is Cuba's most complete colonial city, with great museums and an active *santería* tradition, plus a superb beach close by *(see pp16–17)*.

Jardines del Rey 6

Stretching 275 miles (442 km) along Cuba's northern coastline, this chain of offshore islands and cays is lined with stunning beaches. Three islands offer superb diving plus exciting watersports and deluxe hotels *(see pp18–19)*.

Camagüey 7

The colonial buildings of the "City of Tinajones" are showing their age, but the city is slowly being restored. Rich in history, it is awash with imposing churches looming over cobbled plazas *(see pp20–21)*.

Holguín 8

This provincial capital has played a key role in Cuban history. Its plazas are lined with museums and cultural centers. Castro's birthplace and a beach resort are two of its attractions *(see pp22–3)*.

Santiago de Cuba 9

Santiago de Cuba exudes a mystique that is influenced by its French and Afro-Caribbean associations. Intriguing architecture includes Cuba's oldest building, a fine cathedral, plus numerous key sites and monuments relating to the Revolution *(see pp24–5)*.

Baracoa 10

Founded in 1511 as Cuba's first city, Baracoa enjoys a stupendous setting backed by rainforest-clad mountains. A buzzing street life, scenic mountain hikes, and the Castillo de Seboruco, a castle-turned-hotel, are this town's key attractions *(see pp26–27)*.

TOP 10 Habana Vieja, Havana

With almost 1,000 buildings of historic importance, this intimate quarter is perhaps the largest and most complete colonial complex in the Americas. Like a peopled "museum" full of animated street life, Old Havana boasts an astonishing wealth of castles, cathedrals, convents, palaces, and other important buildings spanning five centuries. An ongoing restoration program, now in its third decade, has transformed the finest structures into museums, hotels, restaurants, boutiques, and trendy bars. Easily walkable, the cobbled plazas and the narrow, shaded streets of Habana Vieja exude colonial charm.

Sculpture, Museo Nacional de Bellas Artes

🕐 **Plaza de Armas' used-book market sells antiquarian editions and collections of Cuban stamps.**

• *Catedral de La Habana: Map X4; opening times vary*
• *Palacio de los Capitanes Generales: Map X4; Plaza de Armas; adm CUC$3*
• *Plaza de Armas: Map X4*
• *Calle Obispo: Map W5–X5*
• *Iglesia y Convento San Francisco: Map X5; Calle Oficios; adm CUC$2*
• *Calle Mercaderes: Map X5*
• *Plaza Vieja: Map X5*
• *Museo de la Revolución: Map W4; Calle Refugio & Agramonte; adm CUC$5*
• *Museo Nacional de Bellas Artes: Map V4; Cuban section & International section: adm CUC$5, CUC$8 for both Cuban and International sections*
• *Parque Histórico-Militar Morro-Cabaña: Map X1; Habana del Este; adm CUC$4*

Top 10 Features

1. Catedral de La Habana
2. Palacio de los Capitanes Generales
3. Plaza de Armas
4. Calle Obispo
5. Iglesia y Convento San Francisco
6. Calle Mercaderes
7. Plaza Vieja
8. Museo de la Revolución
9. Museo Nacional de Bellas Artes
10. Parque Histórico-Militar Morro-Cabaña

1 Catedral de La Habana

Dominating a cobbled plaza, this cathedral *(center)* is graced by an exquisite Baroque façade with asymmetrical bell towers. The restored interior features fine murals.

2 Palacio de los Capitanes Generales

This former governor's palace currently houses the City Museum. Displays of colonial treasures in lavishly decorated hallways and chambers recall the height of Spanish power *(right)*.

3 Plaza de Armas

Habana Vieja's largest cobbled square – the seat of the Spanish government – is the site of the city's first castle *(left)*, the governor's mansion, and the natural history museum.

Most sights are open 10am–5pm on weekdays and 10am–2pm on Sunday.

4 Calle Obispo

This pedestrian-only thoroughfare is lined with book shops, eclectic stores *(left)*, art galleries, and a coin museum.

5 Iglesia y Convento San Francisco

Rising over Plaza de San Francisco, this 17th-century convent is now a splendid religious museum, while the church is a venue for concerts.

6 Calle Mercaderes

This cobbled street links Calle Obispo to Plaza Vieja. Lined with tiny museums, exquisite boutiques, colonial mansions *(below)*, and other attractions, it offers hours of exploration.

7 Plaza Vieja

The fountain at the heart of Old Havana's largest plaza is an exact replica of the 17th-century original. More modern sites here include a brew-pub, a boutique, and intimate museums and galleries.

8 Museo de la Revolución

This vast museum *(left)* in the former Presidential Palace recognizes the growth of Socialism, with a whole section dedicated to Che Guevara.

9 Museo Nacional de Bellas Artes

The fine arts museum is housed in two buildings and displays both an international collection and Cuban art *(see p36)*.

Parque Histórico-Militar Morro-Cabaña 10

Completed in 1774 as the largest fortress in the Americas, the Cabaña fortress *(above)* offers dramatic views across the harbor to Habana Vieja. The Morro castle nearby has a museum on Columbus' voyages.

The City Walls

Havana's fortified city walls were completed in 1697 and encircled the original colonial city. The 30-ft (9-m) high wall was protected by nine bastions and a moat. However, by the early 19th century the city was bursting at the seams. This rapid expansion led to the eventual tearing down of the wall in 1863. Today only fragments of the original wall remain.

The Modern City, Havana

Beyond Habana Vieja, this lively, colorful metropolis of two million people is remarkable for its architecturally significant districts in various stages of dilapidation. Radiating inland from the harbor and coastline like a Spanish fan, the city emerges from compact 19th-century barrios into more spacious 20th-century municipios and post-Revolutionary working class suburbs. Functional apartment blocks give way to once-noble, upper-class districts full of Beaux Arts, Art Deco, and Modernist mansions, while concrete office blocks, government buildings, and hotels from the 1950s lend the city a retro feel.

Rumba dancer at the Teatro Nacional

🎭 To learn Cuban dance steps and enjoy live music, head to the Teatro Nacional.
📞 (7) 879 3558

• *Capitolio: Map V5; Paseo de Martí & Calle Brasil; (7) 861 5519; open 9am–7pm; adm CUC$3*
• *Parque Central: Map V5*
• *Paseo de Martí: Map W1–2*
• *Malecón: S1–W1*
• *Avenida de los Presidentes: Map T1–2*
• *Hotel Nacional: Map U1; Calle O & Calle 21; (7) 836 3564*
• *Cementerio Colón: Map S3; Avenida Zapata & Calle 12; (7) 830 4517; open 8am–5pm daily; adm CUC$1, cameras & guided tours CUC$5*
• *Plaza de la Revolución: Map T3*
• *Universidad de La Habana: Map U2; Calle L & San Lázaro; (7) 878 3231; open 8am–6pm Mon–Fri, closed Jul–Aug*

Top 10 Features

1. Capitolio
2. Parque Central
3. Paseo de Martí
4. Malecón
5. Avenida de los Presidentes
6. Hotel Nacional
7. Cementerio Colón
8. Plaza de la Revolución
9. Universidad de La Habana
10. Miramar

Capitolio

A replica of Washington D.C.'s Capitol *(below)*, this Neo-Classical structure was once a congressional building. The diamond inset in the floor is the point from which all distances are measured in Cuba.

Paseo de Martí

Sloping from Parque Central to the Malecón, this tree-shaded boulevard – known colloquially as Prado – is a great place to meet locals. The area is full of school kids at play during the day *(right)*.

Parque Central

This attractive park makes a good starting point for exploring the city. Featuring a statue of national hero José Martí and surrounded by hotels and several city attractions, it also hosts a lively debate among baseball fanatics.

Malecón

4 Stretching west from the foot of Prado, the Malecón – Havana's seafront boulevard – is lined with eclectic apartment blocks and Mafia-era hotels.

Avenida de los Presidentes

5 Flanked by mansions, this broad boulevard slopes north to the Malecón and is studded with busts and monuments to deceased heroes *(right)* and heads of state.

Hotel Nacional

6 A grandiose legacy of the 1930s, this landmark building *(center)* is modeled on The Breakers, in Palm Beach, Florida. A great place to stay, it boasts an international *Who's Who* list of past guests.

Cementerio Colón

7 Laid out in a regular grid, Havana's huge cemetery *(above)* features an astonishing collection of elaborate tombs. Many of Cuba's most famous personalities are buried here.

Plaza de la Revolución

8 A vast, austere square surrounded by government buildings such as the Ministry of the Interior *(right)*, this square is the heart of state affairs and best visited during the May Day Parade.

Universidad de La Habana

9 With a dramatic Neo-Colonial façade reached via a vast staircase, Havana University's museums showcase Cuba's flora, fauna, and pre-Columbian cultures.

Miramar

10 This sprawling region of western Havana, developed in the 20th century, features avenues lined with mansions and modern deluxe hotels set amid age-old fig trees.

Biotech Success

One of the world's most advanced biotechnology and genetic engineering industries is concentrated in western Havana's district of Siboney. The research facilities here are cutting edge in the field and treatments for illnesses such as cancer, AIDS, and meningitis have been developed.

🔟 Cordillera de Guaniguanico

The pine-clad mountains that begin a short distance west of Havana and run through northern Pinar del Río province are a nature lover's paradise of protected national parks sheltering endangered animals. The mountains grow more rugged westward, where dramatic rock formations called mogotes *tower over lush valleys where tobacco plants thrive in the rich red soils and gentle climate. Centered on a village that itself is a National Historic Monument, the Valle de Viñales is rural Cuba at its most quintessential. Huge caverns beneath the* mogotes *provide a realm of possibilities for spelunkers.*

A shed used to dry tobacco in Pinar del Río

⊘ The 20 mile (32 km) route through the Valley San Carlos, west of Viñales, has awesome scenery.

• Soroa: Map C2; (48) 52 3534; adm CUC$3, includes obligatory guide.
• Las Terrazas: Map C2; Autopista Habana-Pinar del Río, km 51; (48) 57 8600
• Cueva del Indio: Map B2; Carretera Viñales-San Vicente; (48) 79 6280; open 9am–5pm; adm CUC$5
• San Diego de los Baños: Map C2; Balneario San Diego: Calle 23; (48) 54 8880; adm
• Cueva de los Portales: Map C2; Parque Nacional La Güira, La Palma; open 8am–5pm; adm CUC$1
• Viñales: Map B2
• Parque Nacional de Viñales: Map B2
• Gran Caverna de San Tomás: Map B2; open 9am–4pm; adm CUC$8

Top 10 Features

1. Soroa
2. Las Terrazas
3. Cueva del Indio
4. San Diego de los Baños
5. Cueva de los Portales
6. Viñales
7. Parque Nacional de Viñales
8. Tobacco Farms
9. Hiking
10. Gran Caverna de San Tomás

1 Soroa
A lush retreat within the Sierra del Rosario Biosphere Reserve, Soroa *(center)* is famous for Orquideario – its hillside orchid garden – and scenic trails. Enjoy treatments in a bathhouse directly fed by the fresh mineral springs.

2 Las Terrazas
Built as a model rural community and located on the edges of a lake *(left)*, this mountain village is a center for ecotourism and is known for its artists' studios and trails that lead to beautiful waterfalls and coffee farms.

3 Cueva del Indio
Deep inside a *mogote*, this huge cavern lit by artificial lighting has fabulous dripstone formations. After walking a floodlit trail, visitors can ride through an underground river on a motorized boat *(right)*.

San Diego de los Baños
This venerable yet decrepit village was once the most important spa town in Cuba, thanks to its sulphurous springs. The Balneario San Diego still offers therapeutic treatments in a modern facility.

Cueva de los Portales
At an amazing height of 100 ft (30 m), this cavern was Che Guevara's headquarters during the Cuban Missile Crisis. It features Che's old iron bed as well as giant stalagmites and stalactites.

Viñales
Harking back to a bygone era, this quintessentially colonial village exudes unspoiled charm. Ox-carts plod through quiet streets lined with traditional homes fronted by old-fashioned arcades.

Parque Nacional de Viñales
This exquisite valley, the most scenic setting in Cuba, is remarkable for its limestone formations called *mogotes* (*above*). Many of these massive structures are riddled with caves.

Tobacco Farms
The valleys of Pinar del Río are renowned as centers for the production of the nation's finest tobacco, often seen drying in sheds (*below*). The fields are tilled by ox-drawn ploughs even today.

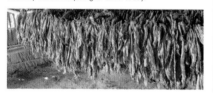

Mogotes
These round-topped rock formations are the remains of a limestone plateau. Over millions of years, water dissolved the rock, creating underground caverns. The ceilings eventually collapsed, leaving free-standing pillars – the *mogotes*. Visit the Mural de la Prehistoria at Valle de Viñales, painted on the face of a *mogote* by artist Diego Rivera.

Hiking
Las Terrazas, Soroa, and Viñales have official trails. Those at Reserva Biosfera de la Península de Guanahacabibes provide a chance to spot endangered species.

Gran Caverna de San Tomás
Take a guided tour through Cuba's largest cave system, with 28 miles (45 km) of galleries adorned with stalactites and stalagmites.

Zapata Peninsula

Protected within a huge biosphere reserve, the Zapata Peninsula is covered in swampland and forests teeming with wildlife. The coast, in turn, is lined with sandy beaches and coral reef, attracting scuba divers. Much of the population here works as carboneros, eking out a living making charcoal. The area is known for Bahía de Cochinos, site of the Bay of Pigs Invasion (see p31). Known locally as "La Victoria", the event is commemorated in two museums.

Top 10 Features

1. Museo Memorial Comandancia FAR
2. Parque Nacional Zapata
3. Laguna del Tesoro
4. Crocodile Farm
5. Fishing
6. Birding
7. Scuba Diving
8. Cenote de los Peces
9. Caleta Buena
10. Museo Girón

A turtle at Caleta Buena

○ The Colibrí restaurant at Boca de Guamá serves delicious crocodile meat, lobster dishes, and good mojitos.

- Map E–F3
- Museo Memorial Comandancia FAR: (45) 91 2504; open 9am–5pm Tue–Sat, 8am–noon Sun; adm CUC$1, cameras CUC$1, guide CUC$1
- Parque Nacional Zapata: (45) 98 7249; adm CUC$10
- Laguna del Tesoro: Boats depart Boca at 10am and noon
- Crocodile farm: (45) 91 5666; open 9am–5:30pm; adm CUC$5
- Cenote de los Peces: open 9am–5pm; adm CUC$1
- Caleta Buena: open 10am–6pm; adm CUC$12
- Museo Girón: (45) 98 4122; open 8am–5pm; adm CUC$2; camera CUC$1; guide CUC$1

Museo Memorial Comandancia FAR

Housed in the former administrative offices of the now defunct Central Australia sugar factory, this museum's exhibits *(below)* recall the Bay of Pigs Invasion in 1961, when Fidel Castro set up his headquarters here.

Parque Nacional Zapata

This vast wetland eco-system can be explored through guided tours and boat trips. The mangrove forests, grasslands, and wild lagoons are home to crocodile and waterfowl.

Laguna del Tesoro

Accessed via a 3-mile (5-km) canal, Treasure Lake is named for the gold that Taíno Indians supposedly hid in its waters when Spanish *conquistadores* arrived. Boat tours *(below)* visit a recreated Taíno village on an island that also hosts a mosquito-ridden resort hotel.

4 Crocodile Farm
Visitors can photograph crocodiles *(above)* from an observation point overlooking the Boca de Guamá, which is Cuba's largest crocodile farm.

5 Fishing
The saltwater shallows off southern Zapata teem with bonefish, a feisty species, while tarpon and the bizarre-looking *manjuari* (alligator gar) inhabit the estuaries of the Hatiguanico river and its tributaries.

6 Birding
Eighteen of Cuba's 22 bird species *(see p50)* inhabit Zapata, including *tocororo* and *zunzuncito* (below). Flamingos tip-toe around Las Salinas lagoon, while sandhill cranes throng the reeds.

7 Scuba Diving
Unspoiled coral reefs *(left)* and a wall plunging 1,000 ft (305 m) lie close to the shore. Inland is a series of *cenotes* – pit-caves full of fresh water – that are suitable for experienced divers only.

9 Caleta Buena
This splendid cove with coral-filled turquoise waters is perfect for snorkeling and scuba diving. White sands top the coral shoreline.

8 Cenote de los Peces
With peacock-blue waters, this exquisite natural pool is 33 ft (10 m) deep, and has a side tunnel that descends 230 ft (70 m). Named for the fish that swim in it, this is a popular spot for cave diving enthusiasts.

10 Museo Girón
Housing military hardware, including tanks and a Cuban air force plane *(right)*, this museum features items relating to the Bay of Pigs invasion and the three-day battle that followed.

La Victoria
Trained by the CIA, the anti-Castro exiles who landed at the Bay of Pigs on April 17, 1961 intended to link up with counter-revolutionaries in the Escambray Mountains. The site was ill-chosen as the landing craft grounded on reefs. The invasion was doomed when President John F. Kennedy refused to authorize the US naval and air support.

For tourist information, contact the Zapata Cubatur office, Villa Playa Girón, (45) 98 4110.

TOP 10 Trinidad

Founded in 1514 by Diego Velázquez, Trinidad was declared a UNESCO World Heritage site in 1988. During the 17th and 18th centuries, the city was a wealthy slave-trading center and hub of sugar production and its wealthy landowners and merchants erected fine homes and mansions. The cobblestone streets lined with pastel-colored houses have barely changed since the colonial era; Trinidad feels like a town that time has passed by. Unlike most Cuban cities, Trinidad sits on a hill and is cooled by near-constant breezes.

A local on a donkey

Playa Ancón

🐷 Locals have many scams to get you to stay at specific *casas particulares*. Don't trust any tout telling you that your choice of hotel has closed.

🍴 Paladar Estela serves great meals out in an intimate, tree-shaded courtyard *(see p125).*

• Map H4
• Museo Romántico: Calle Echerri & Calle Bolívar; (41) 99 4363; open 9am–5pm Tue–Sun; adm CUC$2, cameras CUC$1
• Museo Histórico: Calle Bolívar 423; (41) 99 4460; open 9am–5pm Sat–Thu; 9am–1pm Sun; adm CUC$2, cameras CUC$1
• Antiguo Convento de San Francisco de Asís: Calle Echerri 59; (41) 99 4121; open 9am–5pm Tue–Sun; adm CUC$1
• Casa de la Trova: Calle Echerri 29; (41) 99 6445; open 9am–2am; adm CUC$1 after 8pm.

Top 10 Features

1. Plaza Mayor
2. Museo Romántico
3. Museo Histórico
4. Antiguo Convento de San Francisco de Asís
5. Casa de la Trova
6. Shopping
7. Nightlife
8. Playa Ancón
9. La Boca
10. Casas Particulares

Plaza Mayor
This atmospheric, palm-shaded square *(above)* at the heart of the old city is surrounded by a cathedral and important mansions that today house museums and art galleries.

Museo Romántico
The Palacio Brunet, now a museum, is furnished in period style *(right).* The beautiful architectural details include a carved cedar ceiling and *mediopuntos* – half-moon stained-glass windows.

Museo Histórico
Housed in the Palacio Cantero, this museum's exhibits, including a fountain that once spouted *eau de cologne,* tell the town's history.

Vehicular traffic is not permitted in the restored heart of the colonial city around Plaza Mayor.

4 Antiguo Convento de San Francisco de Asís

This ancient convent *(center)* hosts a museum that recounts the fight against counter-revolutionaries *(see p31)*. The landmark bell-tower can be climbed for a commanding view of the historic center.

5 Casa de la Trova

Traditional music is played at the "House of the Trou-bador," *(below)* on Plazuela de Segarte. This 1777 man-sion is adorned with murals.

6 Shopping

Good bargains can be found at the crafts markets lining the streets *(below)*, where locals sell ceramic wind-chimes and papier mâché models of 1950s US automobiles.

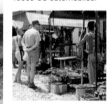

7 Nightlife

Trinidad is rightly celebrated for its after-dark ambience and parti-cularly for its traditional performances by Afro-Cuban troupes.

8 Playa Ancón

This is an immaculate beach with turquoise waters on a peninsula 6 miles (10 km) from Trinidad. It is the setting for three tourist hotels.

10 Casas Particulares

Many *casas particulares (see p127)* are atmospheric colonial properties full of exquisite antiques and often just steps away from the main plazas.

9 La Boca

This rocky beach *(below)* has spectacular views of the Escambray mountains. Shaded by *flamboyán* trees, the sands are a great place to mingle with the locals.

Steam Trains

About 100 steam trains still operate in Cuba. Most are used to haul sugarcane to the mills, while a few are used for tourist excursions. Many trains date back to more than a century. Maintenance is an ongoing problem – every year several trains are abandoned.

For tourist information, contact the Trinidad Cubatur office, Calle Maceo and Simón Bolívar 352, (41) 99 6368.

Top 10 Jardines del Rey

Rising from the Atlantic sea along the north shore of Ciego de Ávila and Camagüey provinces, this 280-mile (450-km) long archipelago, known as the King's Garden, contains hundreds of islands. Three of the major cays are linked to the mainland by pedraplenes (causeways), although only Cayo Coco and neighboring Cayo Guillermo have tourist facilities. Lined with white sandy beaches melting into clear, warm turquoise waters, these twin isles are popular with package vacationers. Flamingos wander the inshore lagoons, while other birds inhabit a nature reserve. Unfortunately, the causeway to Cayo Coco blocks ocean currents, much to the detriment of marine ecology.

A classic American auto, often available to rent

The cays were once reserved for tourists, but now Cubans can also access them. If arriving in a rental car, you will need your passport for the police checkpoints, where you could be searched for Cuban stowaways.

There are few places to eat outside the resort hotels. Sitio La Güira, (33) 30 1208, open 9am–9pm daily, serves food in a countryside setting 8 miles (12 km) from Cayo Guillermo.

• Playa Flamingo: Map K2
• Cayo Guillermo: Map K2
• Parque Nacional El Bagá: Map K2; (33) 30 1063; open 9:30am–5pm; guided tour: CUC$19–$25
• Boat Adventure: (33) 30 1515; adm CUC$41
• Pedraplén: Map K2
• Cayo Sabinal: Map M3
• Cayo Coco: Map K2

Top 10 Features

1. Playa Flamingo
2. Cayo Guillermo
3. Flamingos
4. Water Sports
5. Parque Nacional El Bagá
6. Boat Adventure
7. Pedraplén
8. Cayo Sabinal
9. Horseback Riding
10. Sol Meliá Beach Hotels

Playa Flamingo
This lovely strip of white sand *(above)* stretching for 3 miles (5 km) is one of Cuba's most beautiful beaches and remains unclaimed by giant hotels. The turquoise waters are shallow enough for wading up to 200 m (650 ft) from the shore.

Cayo Guillermo
Connected to Cayo Coco by a raised highway, this island *(center)* is lined with pretty beaches shelving into the waters. Mangroves grow in the channel that separates the two islands. Dunes reach 59 ft (18 m) at Playa Pilar.

Flamingos
Graceful flamingos *(right)* flock to the Laguna de los Flamencos from every April to November. Parador La Silla is the best place to spot them flying overhead at sunrise and dusk.

5 Parque Nacional El Bagá

Studded with lakes surrounded by mangroves and juniper forest, this park's highlights are its nature trail, iguanas, hutias, and a crocodile enclosure.

4 Water Sports

The resort hotels offer a wide range of beach and ocean activities, including banana-boat rides and catamarans *(above)*. Excellent visibility reveals an exciting underwater world for snorkelers and divers.

6 Boat Adventure

Although billed as an "eco-tour," this fun excursion into the mangroves is by way of noisy jet-skis *(above)* that usually scare the birds away.

7 Pedraplén

The highway linking Cayo Coco to the mainland runs ruler-straight across the Bahía de Perros, slicing it in two. At its north end, the road weaves through a series of small islands with herons, roseate spoonbills, and other wading birds.

8 Cayo Sabinal

This virginal island's beaches *(above)* are fringed by a coral reef. Wild pigs inhabit the scrub-covered isle, and flamingos, the inshore lagoons.

9 Cayo Coco

With miles of sandy beaches, Cayo Coco is a haven for marine birds and a popular destination for families, divers, and water sports enthusiasts.

Hemingway and the Cays

During World War II, Ernest Hemingway patrolled off the north coast of Cuba in his sportfishing vessel, *Pilar*. While searching for Nazi submarines in Jardines del Rey, he encountered a U-boat, which then escaped. His experiences were the basis for his novel, *Islands in the Stream*.

10 Sol Meliá Beach Hotels

Spain's Sol Meliá has 24 hotels in Cuba, including five on Cayo Coco and Cayo Guillermo *(see p133)*, that offer a plethora of restaurants, water sports, and creature comforts *(right)*.

 For tourist information, contact the Jardines del Rey Cubatur office, Cayo Coco, Ciego de Ávila, (33) 30 1436.

🔟 Camagüey

A cradle of Cuban culture, the "City of Tinajones" lies in the heart of cattle country and was laid out with irregular streets designed as a convoluted maze to thwart pirates. The historic center is full of well-preserved colonial plazas and cobbled streets featuring antique churches and convents, and by colorful 17th- and 18th-century domestic buildings featuring red-tile roofs, lathe-turned wooden window grills, and spacious interior courtyards adorned with the city's trademark oversized jars called tinajones.

Bronze statue of
Ignacio Agramonte

Teatro Principal

🕐 Watch out for the *jineteros* (hustlers) looking to guide visitors to a *casa particular (see p127)*.

🍴 El Ovejito *(see p103)* on Calle Hermanos Agüero stands out for its lamb dishes.

• Map L2
• Museo Ignacio Agramonte: Av. de los Mártires; (32) 28 2425; open 10am–4pm Tue–Sat, 10am–1pm Sun; adm CUC$1
• Catedral Nuestra Señora de la Merced: Parque Agramonte; (32) 29 4965
• Teatro Principal: Calle Padre Valencia; (32) 29 3048
• Iglesia Nuestra Señora de la Soledad: Av. República & Agramonte
• Iglesia Sagrado Corazón de Jesús: Parque Martí
• Casa Natal Ignacio Agramonte: Calle Agramonte 459; (32) 29 7116; open 9am–5pm Tue–Sat, 8am–noon Sun; adm CUC$2

Top 10 Features

1. Parque Agramonte
2. Plaza San Juan de Dios
3. Plaza del Carmen
4. Museo Ignacio Agramonte
5. Catedral Nuestra Señora de la Merced
6. Teatro Principal
7. Iglesia Nuestra Señora de la Soledad
8. Iglesia Sagrado Corazón de Jesús
9. Casa Natal Ignacio Agramonte
10. Ballet de Camagüey

Parque Agramonte
Dominated by a bronze equestrian statue of Ignacio Agramonte, the town's main square is surrounded by interesting colonial buildings, including the 18th-century cathedral with a six-story bell tower.

Plaza San Juan de Dios
A national monument, this plaza is lined by 18th-century pastel buildings *(left)* that reflect the local style. On the east side, a former church and military hospital houses a museum of colonial architecture.

Plaza del Carmen
Graced by a restored Baroque convent that functions as an art gallery, this cobblestone plaza is pedestrianized and features life-size ceramic figures of locals depicted in daily pursuits *(right)*.

Museo Ignacio Agramonte
This eclectic museum housed in the former Spanish cavalry headquarters focuses on local and natural history *(above)* and boasts a fabulous collection of art.

Catedral Nuestra Señora de la Merced
Dating from 1748, this Baroque church features noteworthy murals and the Santa Sepulcro, a statue of Christ in a coffin cast from 23,000 silver coins.

Teatro Principal
This Neo-Classical theater (1850) was rebuilt in 1926. Its marble staircase is lit by a gilt chandelier. It is the principal venue for the acclaimed Ballet de Camagüey.

Iglesia Nuestra Señora de la Soledad
Built in 1776, this fine example of Cuban Baroque architecture has a lovely wooden *alfarje* ceiling and decoratively painted pillars *(above)*.

Iglesia Sagrado Corazón de Jesús
This gracious, Neo-Gothic church dating from 1755 has been restored. It has a magnificent wooden ceiling, exquisite frescoes, and an elaborate gilt altar.

Casa Natal Ignacio Agramonte
This former home of a local hero of Cuban Independence displays colonial furniture plus Agramonte's personal belongings, including his pistol. It has an intimate courtyard with *tinajones*.

Ballet de Camagüey
Second only to Havana's Ballet National, Camagüey's globally acclaimed troupe *(right)*, founded in 1967, has toured over 40 countries. In season, it performs at the Teatro Principal.

Tinajones
Large earthenware jars up to 6 ft (2 m) wide called *tinajones* are a symbol of Camagüey. Introduced by Catalonian immigrants in the early 1700s, they are used to collect rainwater as well as for decorative purposes in courtyards and gardens.

For tourist information, contact the Camagüey Cubatur office, Calle Ignacio Agramonte 421, (32) 25 4785.

Holguín

This sprawling industrial city, known as the "City of Squares", radiates around a compact colonial core arranged in an easily navigated grid. Its numerous historic plazas include Parque Calixto García, named for the general who liberated the city from the Spanish in 1872. With its abundance of small museums, Holguín has an especially active cultural life. Tourists generally bypass the town to visit the hilltop tourist complex of Mirador de Mayabe or the beach resort of Guardalavaca, offering various ecological and archaeological attractions as well as spectacular scuba diving.

Hacha de Holguín

Steps to Loma de la Cruz

⭐ During May, Holguín bustles with events during Semana de la Cultura Holguinera.

🍺 Taberna Pancho *(see p113)* on Avenida Dimitriov serves draft beer and pork and shrimp dishes.

• Map N4
• Casa Natal de Calixto García: Frexes & Miró; (24) 42 5610; open 9am–5pm Tue–Sat, 10am–6pm Sun; adm CUC$1
• Museo Provincial: Calle Frexes 198; (24) 46 3395; open 8:30am–4:30pm Tue–Sat, 8:30am–noon Sun; adm CUC$1, cameras CUC$1
• Playa Guardalavaca: map P5
• Chorro de Maíta: Carretera Guardalavaca-Banes; (24) 43 0201; open 9am–5pm Tue–Sun, 9am–1pm Mon; adm CUC$2
• Mirador de Mayabe: Valle de Mayabe; (24) 42 2160; open 10am–6pm; adm CUC$10; entrance includes CUC$8 for drinks and snacks

Top 10 Features

1. Plaza Calixto García
2. Museo Provincial
3. Plaza San José
4. Loma de la Cruz
5. Plaza de la Marqueta
6. Casa de la Trova
7. Playa Guardalavaca
8. Chorro de Maíta
9. Mirador de Mayabe
10. Gibara

Plaza Calixto García
This large, tree-shaded plaza features the marble monument of General Calixto García *(above)*. The busy square is home to the city's main museums, including Casa Natal de Calixto García, where the hero was born.

Museo Provincial
The Neo-Classical building that houses this musem used to be a social club for the Spanish elite. Displays include historical artifacts, most notably the Hacha de Holguín – a pre-Columbian stone axe carved with human motifs.

Plaza San José
An antique, cobbled square, this is the most intimate of the city's plazas and a pleasant place to sit on benches beneath shady trees. Surrounded by colonial buildings, it is home to the Iglesia de San José, which is topped by a domed clocktower *(left)*.

4 Loma de la Cruz

With views over the town, this hill is named for the Holy Cross at its summit and can be reached via 485 steps. It is the site for the Romerias de Mayo pilgrimage every May.

5 Plaza de la Marqueta

The ruins of a former market stand over this partially-restored plaza, which features life-sized bronze figures *(left)*. It is lined with many shops including the Cuban Book Institute's Linotype print shop.

6 Casa de la Trova

This is one of Cuba's liveliest music venues *(below)* with two programs daily. It is named for Faustino Oramas "El Guayabero" Osorio, an octogenarian who still plays the guitar here *(see p17)*.

7 Playa Guardalavaca

A one-hour drive northeast of Holguín, this resort is lined with wonderful beaches and unspoiled coral reefs that tempt diving enthusiasts.

9 Mirador de Mayabe

Offering a stunning vista over the Mayabe valley, this lookout is the setting for a fine hotel, a country-style restaurant, and a cliff-top pool. A recreated Cuban farmstead is famous for its beer-drinking donkey.

8 Chorro de Maíta

This burial place, Cuba's largest pre-Columbian Indian site *(below)*, is an archaeological treasure with skeletons next to funerary offerings. Adjacent to it is a re-created Indian village called Aldea Taína.

Organs

The Fábrica de Órganos at Carretera a Gibara 301 is the only factory in Cuba still making mechanical hand-driven *órganos pneumáticos* (air-compression organs) using traditional methods. The machines are fed with cards punched with the score. The organs can be heard in Plaza San José on weekends.

10 Gibara

A windswept coastal town, Gibara was once a prominent port protected by a fortress. Packed with colonial buildings, it has several interesting museums, including the Museo de Artes Decorativas *(see p37)*.

For tourist information, contact the Holguín Cubatur office, Guardalavaca, (24) 43 0676.

🔟 Santiago de Cuba

The country's second-oldest and second-largest city has a flavor all its own thanks to it being the most African city in Cuba and the most musical place in the island nation. Surrounded by mountains, Santiago was founded in 1511 on the hilly east shore of a deep flask-shaped bay. Its sloping colonial core is replete with noteworthy historic buildings, while its fascinating past as the first capital of Cuba is enriched by its importance as a hotbed of revolution. Fidel Castro studied here as a youth and later initiated the Revolution with an attack on the Moncada barracks (see p31). Santiago explodes with colorful frenzy during Carnaval each July.

Musicians at Museo Emilio Bacardí

🎵 **Comparsas (Afro-Cuban associations) host music and dance workshops during Carnaval (July).**

🥃 **Sample various rums at the Fábrica de Ron Caney. ✆ (22) 662 5576**

• Map P6
• Cuartel Moncada: Calle General Portuondo; (22) 66 1157; open 9:30am–5:15pm Tue–Sat, 9:30am–12:30pm Sun; adm CUC$2, cameras CUC$1
• Museo Emilio Bacardí: Calle Pío Rosado; (22) 62 8402; open 9am–11:45pm Tue–Sat, 1pm–4:45pm Sun, 1pm–4:45pm Mon; adm CUC$2
• Cementerio Santa Ifigenia: Calzada Crombet; (22) 63 2723; open 7am–6pm; adm CUC$1; cameras CUC$1
• Parque Histórico-Militar El Morro: Carretera al Morro, km 7.5; (22) 69 1569; open 9am–7:30pm; adm CUC$4, cameras CUC$1

Top 10 Features

1. Cuartel Moncada
2. Plaza Dolores
3. Museo Emilio Bacardí
4. Parque Céspedes
5. Calle Heredia
6. Plaza de la Revolución
7. Cementerio Santa Ifigenia
8. Vista Alegre
9. Parque Histórico-Militar El Morro
10. El Cobre

1 Cuartel Moncada
The setting for Castro's attack on July 26, 1953 *(see p30)*, this former military barracks *(above)* is today a school housing the Museo Histórico 26 de Julio recalling the failed venture, as well as a general history of Cuba.

2 Plaza Dolores
This popular tree-shaded plaza *(left)* is a pleasant place to relax. The former Iglesia de Nuestra Señora de los Dolores church on the east side now functions as a venue for classical concerts.

3 Museo Emilio Bacardí

Visitors can view colonial-era armaments, relics from the slave trade, as well as a superlative body of paintings and sculptures in Cuba's oldest museum (above).

4 Parque Céspedes

At the heart of the city, this square is surrounded by historic buildings such as the Casa de Diego Velázquez, and the Catedral de la Asunción (center).

5 Calle Heredia

A lively street, this is the setting for a colorful cultural fair on weekends and is abuzz with bar-life on any other night. The Museo del Carnaval and the Casa de la Trova are among the intriguing attractions found here.

6 Plaza de la Revolución

This vast plaza was used primarily for political rallies and features a huge monument of General Antonio Maceo on horseback (above). There is a hologram museum to the rear.

8 Vista Alegre

A leafy residential district, Vedado features mansions and Modernist homes (below). The Casa del Caribe and Casa de la Cultura Africana honor Afro-Cuban culture.

7 Cementerio Santa Ifigenia

Many important figures are buried at this monumental cemetery (above), including Carlos Manuel de Céspedes and José Martí, whose casket is on view to the public.

Virgen de la Caridad del Cobre

Miraculous powers are ascribed to the Virgin of Charity, Cuba's patron saint, who is represented as a black Virgin Mary holding a black Christ. According to legend, three fishermen were caught in a storm in 1608 and survived because a statue of the Virgin appeared, calming the seas for them.

9 Parque Histórico-Militar El Morro

Guarding the entrance to Santiago Bay, the well-preserved 17th-century El Morro castle offers spectacular coastal vistas. Soldiers in period costume march in and fire a cannon at dusk.

10 El Cobre

This village is famous for Basílica de Nuestra Señora de la Caridad del Cobre, Cuba's most important church, where pilgrims gather to pray to the Virgen del Cobre.

For tourist assistance, contact the Santiago de Cuba Cubatur office, Ave. Victoriano Garzón between 3ra and 4ta, (22) 65 2560.

25

🔟 Baracoa

Tucked inside a broad bay enfolded by mountains, Baracoa sits at the far northeast corner of Cuba. This antique city was founded in 1511 as the island's first settlement. When governor Diego Velázquez later moved to Santiago, a long period of isolation set in. Locals claim that the Bahía de Miel was the site of Columbus' first landing in Cuba in 1492, and that the flat-topped mountain he described is El Yunque, which rises dramatically behind Baracoa. Lined with venerable wooden houses in local, vernacular style, the sleepy town is laid out in a tight grid. A favorite with independent travelers, Baracoa today buzzes with crowds of tourists.

The endangered hutia

🔎 If you are curious to see the endangered rodent-like hutia and insect-eating almique, head to Parque Zoológico, 4 miles (7 km) east of town. ✹ Map R5

🍴 A good place to sample local dishes is Restaurante Duaba in the Hotel El Castillo, which serves unusually creative fare *(see p113)*.

• Map R5
• Fuerte Matachín: Calle Martí; (21) 64 2122; open 8am–noon, 2pm–6pm; adm CUC$1
• Catedral de Nuestra Señora de la Asunción: Plaza Independencia; (21) 64 3352; open 9am–noon, 2pm–5pm
• Museo Arqueológico: open 8am–5pm Mon–Fri, 8am–noon Sat–Sun; CUC$2

Top 10 Features

1. Fuerte Matachín
2. The Cathedral
3. Plaza Independencia
4. Hotel El Castillo
5. Bahía de Baracoa
6. Museo Arqueológico
7. Regional Cuisine
8. El Yunque
9. Hiking
10. Playa Duaba

1 Fuerte Matachín
Guarding the eastern entrance to town, this tiny fortress *(above)* contains the Museo Municipal that traces the history of the region and a collection of *polymites* – colored snails particular to the region.

2 The Cathedral
The Catedral de Nuestra Señora de la Asunción, built in 1512, stands over Plaza Independencia and safeguards the Cruz de la Parra, a wooden cross said to have been brought to Cuba by Columbus.

3 Plaza Independencia
This small triangular plaza – also known as Parque Central – has a bust of the heroic Indian leader Hatuey *(left)*. At night the park bustles with locals who gather to share beer.

Hotel El Castillo

Built to repel the British, the Castillo de Seboruco fortress now houses a hotel *(see p131)* with shimmering views.

Bahía de Baracoa

This flask-shaped bay to the west of town is lined by a gray-sand beach, with the thickly forested Alturas de Baracoa mountains forming a backdrop.

Museo Arqueológico

Full of fascinating drip-stone formations, the Cueva de Paraíso hosts an archaeological museum filled with Taíno Indian artifacts and a funerary cave displaying skeletons in situ *(below)*.

Regional Cuisine

Baracoa is known for its cuisine based on creative use of coconut, such as the *cucurucho*, a coconut dessert mixed with fruits and honey, and *calalú*, a vegetable simmered in coconut milk.

El Yunque

An anvil-shaped mountain formation *(left)*, El Yunque rises above the rain forests that provide a habitat for rare species of flora and fauna.

Playa Duaba

This black-sand beach west of Baracoa features a bust of General Antonio Maceo who landed here in 1895 and fought the first battle of the War of Independence here.

Hiking

Guided hikes into the rain forests to the south of town lead deep into the mountains. Birders still hope to spot the ivory-billed woodpecker, believed to be extinct.

Polymites

The polymita genus of snail, endemic to the Baracoa region, is remarkable for its multi-colored shell with a whorled pattern. Each snail has a unique pattern and color. With a dwindling population, the polymite is now endangered. You are advised not to buy any shells offered for sale.

For tourist information, contact the Baracoa Cubatur office, Calle Maceo 149 esq. Pelayo Cuervo, (21) 64 5306.

One of the Revolutionary Marches of 1959

Moments in History

1 c. 500 BC: Taíno Culture
The Taíno people arrived from the Orinoco region of South America on the island they called Cuba. Worshipping gods of nature, this peaceful society was organized into nuclear villages led by *caciques* (chieftains).

2 1492: Columbus Arrives
The Genoese explorer sighted Cuba during his first voyage and renamed it Juana. In 1509, Columbus' son Diego conquered the island and exterminated the Taínos. Conquistador Diego Velázquez founded the first town, Baracoa, in 1512.

3 1762: The English Occupy Cuba
The golden age of the Spanish colony ended when English troops seized Havana. England opened Cuba to free trade and expanded the slave trade. In 1763, Havana was returned to Spain by the English in exchange for Florida.

4 1868: Ten Years War
Landowner Carlos Manuel de Céspedes freed his slaves and revolted against Spanish rule. A guerrilla war ensued, in which towns were razed and the economy devastated. Later, US companies bought up Cuban sugar plantations.

5 1895: War of Independence
Exiled nationalist José Martí returned to lead the fight for independence. Though martyred in battle, his forces gained the upper hand, but were sidelined after the USS *Maine* was destroyed in Havana harbor. The US declared war on Spain, and invaded Cuba, occupying it.

6 1902: Independence
Following four years of US military rule, Washington granted the island its independence. A period of mostly corrupt government followed, while US corporations came to dominate the Cuban sugar-based economy.

7 1953: Castro Attacks Moncada
Castro launched the Cuban Revolution with an audacious attack timed to coincide with carnival celebrations in Santiago. The assault failed and 64 captured

A depiction of Columbus' arrival in Cuba

Preceding pages **A view of Havana at night**

rebels were tortured to death. Fidel delivered a brilliant defense at his trial, during which he gained national sympathy.

8 1959: Revolution Triumphs
On New Year's Eve 1958, General Fulgencio Batista fled Cuba and Castro delivered a victory speech in Santiago in advance of his triumphant journey to Havana. A newly formed democratic government was quickly usurped by Castro, who allied with the Soviet Union and initiated dramatic reforms.

A triumphant Fidel Castro in 1959

9 1962: Bay of Pigs Invasion
CIA-trained Cuban exiles stormed ashore to assist Cuban-based counter-revolutionaries in toppling Castro. The attack was repelled. Castro took advantage of popular sentiment against the US-inspired invasion to announce that Cuba would be socialist.

10 1991: Período Especial Begins
Thirty years of economic support ended overnight when the Soviet Union collapsed. The economy imploded and Cubans faced extreme hardship, triggering a mass exodus to the US on flimsy rafts. Since 1994, the crisis has eased with a tourism boom helping to promote recovery.

Top 10 National Figures

1 Christopher Columbus (1451–1506)
Visionary Genoese explorer and the first European to sight Cuba on October 27, 1492.

2 Hatuey (died 1512)
Heroic chieftain who led resistance to Spanish rule and was burned at the stake.

3 Carlos Manuel de Céspedes (1819–74)
The "Father of the Homeland" freed his slaves and launched the wars for independence.

4 José Martí (1853–95)
Cuba's foremost national hero, a writer and leader, who was martyred in battle.

5 Máximo Gómez (1836–1905)
Dominican-born general and supreme commander of the Cuban liberation army.

6 Antonio Maceo Grajales (1845–96)
Brilliant guerrilla leader in the independence wars, Grajales was finally killed in battle.

7 Calixto García (1839–98)
Second-in-command of the independence army, and liberator of many Spanish-held cities.

8 Gerardo Machado (1871–1939)
Corrupt military dictator who ruled Cuba with an iron fist between 1924 and 1933.

9 Fulgencio Batista (1901–73)
Mulatto general who seized power in 1934 and ruled Cuba until he fled on New Year's Eve in 1958.

10 Fidel Castro (b.1926)
Former head of state who led the Revolution. Castro held power for five decades.

Left **Complejo Histórico Abel Santamaría** Center **Granjita Siboney** Right **Statue of Che Guevara**

Revolutionary Sites

1 Museo de la Revolución
The struggle for independence, the effort to topple Batista,
and the subsequent building of
Socialism are highlighted in this
museum. Housed in the former
presidential palace, it was built in
1920 and fitted with lavish
interior decoration. The
"Corner of Cretins" pokes
fun at Batista and at
presidents Ronald Reagan
and George Bush *(see p9)*.

2 Granma Memorial
The *Granma*, the
vessel in which Castro
sailed to Cuba with his
guerrilla army, is displayed
within a glass case in
an open-air plaza to
the rear of the
Museo de la
Revolución. Exhibits
at the memorial include
military hardware left over from
the Bay of Pigs invasion. 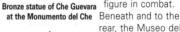 Map V4
• Calle Trocadero, Havana • (7) 862 4091
• Open 9am–5pm daily • Adm

**Bronze statue of Che Guevara
at the Monumento del Che**

3 Presidio Modelo
This model prison,
completed in 1936,
accommodated Fidel and Raúl
Castro as well as 25 other
revolutionaries sentenced to
imprisonment following the
Moncada attack. The hospital
wing where they slept is now a
museum, while Fidel's private
room with its marble
bathroom contains a
collection of the books he
read during his years of
incarceration *(see p81)*.

4 Monumento del Che
A massive bronze figure
of Che Guevara holding his
rifle stands over this
monument, featuring
bas-reliefs of Che's
figure in combat.
Beneath and to the
rear, the Museo del
Che is Cuba's principal museum
dedicated to the Argentinian
revolutionary. His remains are
interred in an adjacent mausoleum *(see p91)*.

5 Museo Camilo Cienfuegos
The small town of
Jaguajay is noted solely
for its museum, which
commemorates the life
of Camilo Cienfuegos,
the revolutionary
commander who won a
victory over Batista's
forces at this site in
1958. The exhibits on

The *Granma* enclosed in a glass case

Museo de la Lucha Clandestina

Left **Castro resting on a bed** Center **Castro's jail cell** Right **The Moncada barracks**

🔟 Moments in Fidel Castro's Life

1 Birth and Childhood
Born on August 13, 1926 to a rural patriarch and his maid at Birán in Holguín, Castro was raised by his mother and was not formally recognized by his father until he turned 17.

2 Jesuit Schooling
Castro was schooled by Jesuits in Santiago de Cuba, and later at Belén college in Havana. Although combative, he excelled in his studies and was named Cuba's top student athlete.

3 University
Castro entered the University of Havana law school in 1945, where he became embroiled in politics as a student leader, and graduated in 1950. He made national headlines several times as an outspoken critic of the government.

Castro as a child

4 Attack on Moncada
After Batista overthrew the constitutional government and cancelled elections in March 1953, Castro initiated a legal petition against him. It failed and he launched his revolution with an assault on the Moncada barracks on July 26, 1953.

5 Prison
After giving his impassioned "History Will Absolve Me" speech in 1953, Castro was sent to prison for 15 years. He used the time to organize his forces. Amnestied in May 1955, he set up a guerrilla army during exile in Mexico.

6 War in the Sierra Maestra
After his exile ended, Castro initiated a plan to return to Cuba. On landing in the Granma province, his forces were ambushed, but Castro, Raúl Castro, and Che Guevara escaped and established their headquarters. Castro directed the opposition from here, winning several battles and slowly taking control of Cuba.

7 Batista Toppled
Castro pledged to support a provisional democratic government after his forces ousted Batista in 1959. Meanwhile, separate guerrilla columns led by Che Guevara and Camilo Cienfuegos won key victories.

Castro at the Sierra Maestra hideout

When Santa Clara fell to Che Guevara's troops on New Year's Eve, 1958, Batista fled the country and Castro triumphantly returned to Havana.

8 Bay of Pigs
A democratic government was founded, but Castro usurped it and initiated dramatic Socialist reforms. This resulted in a massive exodus of Cubans. A group of unhappy exiles, trained by the CIA, landed at the Bay of Pigs on April 16, 1961 to invade Cuba, but were quickly defeated.

Soviet ship during the Cuban Missile Crisis

9 Cuban Missile Crisis
In December 1961, Castro declared Cuba a Marxist-Leninist state. He signed a pact with the Soviet Union, which installed nuclear missiles in Cuba. However, the US President Kennedy demanded their withdrawal. The nations stood at the edge of nuclear war until Soviet President Khrushchev backed down.

10 Castro Resigns
Castro announced on July 31, 2006 that he had an acute intestinal illness. Handing temporary power to Raúl Castro, he underwent surgery and began a long recovery. Castro resigned on February 19, 2008, ending much speculation as to whether he would return to power.

Top 10 Revolutionary Heroes

1 Raúl Castro (1931–)
Younger brother of Fidel, a life-long communist and leader of the armed forces.

2 Camilo Cienfuegos (1932–59)
Chief of Staff in Fidel's guerrilla army.

3 José Antonio Echeverría (1932–57)
Student leader who led an assault on Batista's palace and was later murdered.

4 Che Guevara (1928–67)
Argentinean doctor-turned-revolutionary who was killed while attempting to inspire a revolution in Bolivia.

5 Julio Antonio Mella (1903–29)
The founder of the Cuban Communist Party, he was murdered in Mexico.

6 Jesús Menéndez (1911–48)
Socialist labor agitator who worked on behalf of local sugarcane workers.

7 Frank País (1934–57)
A principal leader in the M-26-7 movement, País was murdered by Batista's police.

8 Abel Santamaría (1925–53)
Castro's probable successor, Santamaría was killed after the Moncada attack.

9 Haydee Santamaría (1931–80)
Abel's sister was captured at Moncada, but managed to survive the torture.

10 Celia Sánchez (1920–80)
Middle-class socialist who ran the supply line for Castro's guerrilla army and later became his secretary.

Left and center **Museo Oscar María de Rojas** Right **Museo Ernest Hemingway**

Museums

1 Museo Nacional de Bellas Artes

This fine arts museum boasts ancient Egyptian, Greek, and Roman art, and the works of European masters. The Cuban section demonstrates the vitality and range of homegrown art, from the colonial period to the contemporary era *(see p9)*.

2 Museo de la Música

Tracing the evolution of Cuban music, this national music archive exhibits a fabulous collection of musical instruments. You can listen to recordings in the record library.

3 Museo de la Ciudad

The museum in Palacio de los Capitanes Generales covers the history of Havana. Exhibits include the city's first cemetery and a Throne Room built for an unrealized visit by the king of Spain. ◈ *Map X1* • *Calle Tacón, Plaza de Armas, Havana* • *(7) 861 5779* • *Open 9am–6pm* • *Adm*

Exhibit at Museo Emilio Bacardí

4 Museo de la Plata

Colonial-era silverwork is celebrated in this museum in one of the city's oldest houses. Upstairs there is a fine display of swords and firearms. ◈ *Map X1* • *Calle Obispo 113, Habana Vieja, Havana* • *(7) 863 9861* • *Open 9:30am–5pm Tue–Sat, 9:30am–1pm Sun* • *Adm*

5 Museo de Artes Decorativas

Lavish furnishings fill this former Beaux Arts residence of a Cuban countess and reveal the tastes of the 19th-century ruling classes – from the French Rococo furniture and 17th-century Italian sculptures to the pink marble, Art Deco bathroom upstairs. ◈ *Map T1–T2* • *Calle 17 502, Vedado, Havana* • *(7) 830 9848* • *Open 10:30am–5pm Tue–Sat* • *Adm*

6 Museo José Martí

A homage to Cuba's foremost 19th-century patriot, this museum is housed in the modest home where the literary genius and independence leader was born. Now a monument, the house exhibits mementos and his original manuscripts. ◈ *Map X2* • *Calle Leonor Pérez 314, Habana Vieja, Havana* • *(7) 861 3778* • *Open 9:30am–4:45pm Tue–Sat, 9:30am–12:45pm Sun* • *Adm*

7 Museo Ernest Hemingway

Finca Vigía, Ernest Hemingway's former home, has been left untouched since his departure from Cuba in 1960. It still contains his books and hunting trophies. His sport-fishing vessel, *Pilar*, sits beneath a pavilion in the garden *(see p68)*.

Unless otherwise stated, visitors to museums are permitted to carry cameras for an additional charge.

Exhibition at Museo José Martí

Museo Oscar María de Rojas

Each of this museum's 14 salons has its own theme, from pre-Columbian culture to the Wars of Independence. Numismatists will enjoy the coin room. The Baroque 19th-century hearse is fascinating, as is the beautifully restored former governor's mansion that hosts the museum. ⊗ *Map F2 • Av 4 Este & Calle Echevarría, Cárdenas • (45) 52 2417 • Open 9am–6pm Tue–Sat, 9am–1pm Sun • Adm*

Museo Emilio Bacardí

Cuba's oldest museum is housed in a Neo-Classical mansion. It boasts relics dating from the pre-Columbian era to the colonial period, and a fine collection related to slavery. Important Cuban art is found upstairs and includes works by Wilfredo Lam *(see p24)*.

Museo de la Guerra Hispano-Cubano-Norteamericano

Situated outside the coastal hamlet of Siboney, this museum recalls the Spanish-American War of 1898, with many of the battle sites located nearby. Exhibits include artillery, torpedoes, uniforms, photographs, and bas-relief maps. ⊗ *Map P6 • Carretera a Siboney, km 13.5 • (22) 39 9119 • Open 9am–5pm Mon–Sat • Adm*

Top 10 Castles

1 Castillo de la Real Fuerza (1582)
Havana's oldest fortress has angular ramparts surrounded by a broad moat. ⊗ *Map X1*

2 El Morro (1603)
This 16th-century castle guards the entrance to Havana harbor. ⊗ *Map X1*

3 Castillo de San Salvador de la Punta (1610)
Designed in conjunction with Havana's El Morro, this castle had the advantage of being able to catch invaders in the crossfire. ⊗ *Map W1*

4 El Morro (1700)
El Morro offers dramatic views at the entrance to Santiago Bay. ⊗ *Map P6*

5 El Castillo (1741)
Baracoa's hilltop castle has served as a prison and is now a hotel. ⊗ *Map R5*

6 Castillo de San Severino (1745)
This small 18th-century castle protected the Matanzas harbor channel. ⊗ *Map E2*

7 Castillo de Jagua (1748)
Guarding Cienfuegos bay, this castle is said to be haunted. ⊗ *Map G3*

8 Fortaleza de la Cabaña (1774)
When completed, this was the largest fortress in the Americas. ⊗ *Map X1*

9 Fuerte Matachín (1802)
Guarding Baracoa from pirates, this castle still has cannons in situ. ⊗ *Map R5*

10 Fuerte de la Loma (1877)
This fort guarded Puerto Padre during the Wars of Independence. ⊗ *Map N4*

Left **A shop selling Santería artifacts** Center **An idol of Eleggua** Right **Batá drums**

🔟 Santería

1 Babalawos
The powerful high priests of *santería* (an Afro-Cuban religion) act as intermediaries to interpret the commands of the *orishas*. They use seashells, coconut husks, and seeds to divine the future and interpret the oracles. A *santero* (aspiring priest) might train for a decade to reach the status of *babalawo*.

2 Santeros
These official practitioners act as priests, healers, and diviners and are sought out by believers for consultations to find solutions to personal problems. *Santeros* are easily identified by their metal bracelets and colorful necklaces, which represent their particular *orisha*.

3 Batá
Of Yoruba origin, the sacred, hourglass-shaped *batá* drums – *itotele*, *iya,* and *okonkolo* – are carved of solid wood. Each of these three styles have a different size and pitch. The drums are used during most important ceremonies and have their own rituals pertaining to their use and care.

4 Orishas
The many deities of *santería* act as intermediaries between human beings and the supreme god,

Olorún. Most *orishas* are avatars of Catholic saints, and each has his or her own costume, colors, symbols, and favorite foods, as well as specific abilities. Each believer has a personal *orisha*, who is considered to have the power over that person's destiny and is worshipped in daily life.

5 Obi
Santería adherents believe that the wisdom of the *orishas* can be divined by dropping four pieces of coconut shell and studying the pattern they form. *Mojubas* (prayers) are said to invite the *orisha* to speak. These *obi* (oracles) are considered to help the believer reach wise decisions. At times, sacred palm seeds or cowrie shells are cast to invoke other oracles.

6 Initiation Ceremonies
Believers who seek a new path in life make a pact of veneration and obedience with their *orisha* through a week-long series of rituals. These require rigid adherence to meet the *orisha's* approval. The final initiation usually involves animal sacrifice. For a year thereafter, the *iyawó* (initiate) adopts strict prescriptions of behavior and dresses solely in white.

An altar for Changó

Santería is a popular Afro-Cuban religion. Most believers have an altar to their orisha in their homes.

Colorful *elekes,* or beads

Elekes

7 These necklaces of colored beads relate to specific *orishas*. While uninitiated believers wear generic *elekes*, the bead patterns are determined by *santeros*, who prepare these necklaces using divination to find an order that reflects the *iyawó's* path.

Ebó

8 Santería rites, known as *ebó*, require offerings of food and drink to the *orishas*. An *ebó* often involves ritual cleansing, and may include sacrificing of chickens, pigeons, or goats. *Ebó* is also used to woo an *orisha's* favor, or guard against witchcraft.

Wemilere

9 These ritual ceremonies are held to honor *orishas*. They comprise prayers, songs, and *batá* drum rhythms. A believer may sometimes go into a trance – he or she is then believed to be possessed by the *orisha*.

Altars

10 Altars are decorated with the attributes of the *orisha*, including their likeness in the form of a doll, devotional objects, and *ebó*. Tiny bells, maracas, and *agogó* (rattles) are played to awaken the *orisha*.

Top 10 Orishas

1 **Olorún**
The principal god, often considered the androgynous sum of all divinity. He is the source of all spiritual energy.

2 **Obatalá**
The father of humankind, he represents wisdom and purity. He is androgynous and celebrates Our Lady of Mercy.

3 **Ochún**
The youngest *orisha*, Ochún is the sensual deity of water as well as the goddess of love.

4 **Yemayá**
The mother goddess is the giver of life and the protector of children and pregnant women.

5 **Changó**
The hot-tempered, heroic god of thunder and lightning represents virility. His symbol is a double-bladed axe.

6 **Babalu Aye**
Associated with disease, Babalu Aye wears rags, walks with a crutch, and is accompanied by his dog.

7 **Eleggua**
God of the crossroads, Eleggua opens or closes the way of life. Cuban drivers often place Eleggua's *elekes* in their cars for protection.

8 **Oggun**
God of metal and war, he fights battles on behalf of petitioners' and is often depicted with a machete.

9 **Osain**
This celibate deity represents the forces of nature. All initiations require his presence.

10 **Oyá**
She controls the fate of the injured and is aligned with the saint, Santa Bárbara.

Left **Portocarrero's** *Escena de Carnaval* Right **Alejo Carpentier**

🔟 Writers and Artists

1 Amelia Peláez (1896–1968)

Influenced by Matisse and Picasso, this ceramist and painter is best known for her vast mural *Carro de la Revolución* (the Revolutionary Car) adorning Hotel Habana Libre *(see p69)*.

2 Wilfredo Lam (1902–82)

Born in Sagua la Grande, Lam befriended many leading European painters while living in Paris. His works strongly reflect Afro-Cuban culture.

3 Alejo Carpentier (1904–80)

Carpentier is known for his cultural journalism focused on Afro-Cuban traditions. He was sent into exile for opposing General Machado. After the Revolution *(see p31)*, he headed Cuba's state publishing house.

Statue of José Martí, Plaza de la Revolucion

4 Dulce María Loynaz (1902–97)

The doyenne of Cuban poetry, Loynaz went into relative seclusion following the Revolution after her husband fled Cuba. Her works were rediscovered in the 1980s, when she re-engaged with literary circles. An erotic intensity infuses many of her works.

Monument to Loynaz in Puerto de la Cruz

5 José Martí (1853–95)

Perhaps the leading Latin American essayist, poet, and journalist of the 19th century, Martí led the Independence movement *(see p30)*. He wrote profusely for the cause of social justice, pan-Americanism, and liberty.

6 Guillermo Cabrera Infante (1929–2005)

This critic, journalist, and novelist is best known for *Tres Tristes Tigres,* his seminal novel about the sordid era of pre-Revolutionary Havana. Post-Revolution, he edited a key literary magazine before being forced into exile for criticizing Castro's government.

7 José Lezama Lima (1910–76)

A gay libertine known as much for his flamboyant lifestyle as for his Baroque writing, Lima was persecuted following the Revolution. Today he ranks

Peláez's *The Tree and the Cross*

among the Cuban literary elite. His most famous work is the semi-biographical *Paradiso*.

Nicolás Guillén (1902–89)

Considered the poet laureate of Cuba, Guillén's African heritage is reflected in his distinctive *poesía negra* (black poetry). He joined the Communist Party at an early age and, following the Revolution, became president of the National Union of Writers and Artists.

René Portocarrero (1912–85)

One of Cuba's masters, Portocarrero is well-represented in Havana's Museo Nacional de Bellas Artes *(see p9)*, his murals are also found in the Teatro Nacional and Hotel Habana Libre. His work is infused with religious icons. ◎ *Map T3 • Teatro Nacional: Paseo y 39; (7) 879 6011; adm*

Manuel Mendive (b. 1944)

Mendive is considered to be Cuba's most visionary and influential living artist. His works are both naive and highly erotic. A practising *santero (see pp38–9)*, Mendive is represented in museums around the world.

Top 10 Famous Cubans

1 Carlos Finlay (1833–1909)
The doctor who discovered that yellow fever is transmitted by mosquitoes.

2 Gerardo Machado (1871–1939)
Corrupt military leader who seized power in 1925 and fled in 1933 *(see p31)*.

3 Fulgencio Batista (1901–73)
A sergeant who carried out a military coup and ran Cuba as a brutal dictator *(see p31)*.

4 José Raúl Capablanca (1888–1942)
The Mozart of chess held the World Chess Championship title from 1921–27.

5 Alberto Díaz Gutiérrez (1928–2001)
This photographer, better known as Korda, shot the iconic image of Che Guevara.

6 Tomás Gutiérrez Alea (1928–96)
A brilliant film-maker, "Titón" was at the forefront of New Latin American cinema.

7 Eligio Sardiñas (1910–88)
Christened "Kid Chocolate" by his fans, this boxing prodigy was also a wild party man.

8 Alicia Alonso (b. 1920)
Cuba's *prima ballerina absoluta* who founded the National Ballet of Cuba.

9 Teófilo Stevenson (b. 1952)
Considered one of the greatest boxers of all time, he refused to turn professional.

10 Ana Fidelia Quirot (b. 1963)
A runner who survived severe burns to win the silver medal at the 1996 Olympics.

Left **A *son* band performing at a café** Right **Timba dance and music**

Musical Styles

1 Danzón
Originating in France via Haiti in the 18th century, *danzón* is the root source of most Cuban music, and gained popularity within slave culture and with Creole peasants. Played by *orquestras típicas*, *danzón* has a repetitive jaunty tempo.

2 Classical
Cuba boasts a National Symphony Orchestra and many smaller accomplished ensembles that are actively sponsored by the government. A unique style has evolved, known as *Afrocubanismo*, incorporating African-derived instruments and rhythms into classical themes.

Tres, a small guitar

3 Jazz
A musical form that has made a resounding comeback in Cuba, jazz was suppressed following the Revolution *(see p31)*. A colorful and fast-paced Afro-Cuban style has emerged, propelling Cuban musicians to the fore of the world jazz scene.

4 Son
Son became popular in the second half of the 19th century in the eastern province of Oriente. Its popularity peaked in the 1950s and was revived decades later after the success of the *Buena Vista Social Club* movie and album.

5 Changüí
A rougher, choppier variant of *son*, *changüí* has minimal instrumentation with the *tres* and *bongos* dominating. It is played mainly in the eastern provinces, notably by groups like the Estrellas Campesinas and Grupo Changüí.

6 Guaguancó
Born in the slave *barracoons* of 18th-century sugar estates, this folkloric Afro-Cuban dance is highly flirtatious. Accompanied by complex bongo rhythms, the male dancer circles his female partner, who dances in a provocative yet defensive manner in front of him.

An Afro-Cuban jazz trio

Salsa dancers

Top 10 Musicians

1 Chucho Valdés (b. 1941)
This Grammy award-winning jazz pianist is considered to be one of the world's greats.

2 Compay Segundo (1907–2003)
Sentimental guitarist of the 1940s, Segundo resurrected his career with the *Buena Vista Social Club.*

3 Frank Fernández (b. 1944)
Cuba's foremost classical pianist studied at Moscow's Tchaikovsky Conservatory.

4 Celia Cruz (1925–2003)
Legendary salsa singer who left Cuba in 1960 and found fame in the US.

5 Benny Moré (1919–63)
This tenor sang everything from *son* to *mambo* and is considered perhaps the greatest Cuban singer of all.

6 Juan Formell (b. 1942)
Founder of Orquesta Revé and Los Van Van – Cuba's most popular salsa band.

7 Silvio Rodríguez (b. 1946)
The foremost exponent of politicized *nueva trova* ballads, also a former member of parliament.

8 Gonzalo Rubalcalda (b. 1963)
This contemporary jazz pianist often tours the world and is a Grammy award winner.

9 Pablo Milanés (b. 1943)
A singer-songwriter of *nueva trova*, this guitarist hails from the city of Bayamo.

10 Rubén González (1919–2003)
A jazz pianist, González first performed in 1940 and starred in *Buena Vista Social Club.*

7 Salsa
A popular form that evolved in the 1960s, when Cuban musicians began experimenting with new sounds and styles from the US. Fusing jazz and rock with traditional *son*, it is normally fast and intense, but can also be slow and romantic.

8 Rumba
Social gatherings in Cuba often evolve into informal *rumbas*, a generic term which covers a variety of African-derived rhythms and dances involving sensuous flicks of the hips. Many rumbas involve a call and answer pattern between singers and drummers.

9 Timba
A derivative of salsa, the highly aggressive and innovative *timba* is an eclectic and ever-evolving musical form that incorporates various genres, including classical, disco, and even hip hop. Improvization is key to this flexible form.

10 Rap
Cuba's contemporary rap scene differs markedly from its aggressive US counterpart. *Raperos* adopted rap to express their frustrations and lyrics that focus on socio-political commentary with the intention of bettering society.

The Buena Vista Social Club (1999) *is a documentary-film that highlights the work of* son *musicians over 80 years old.*

Swimming with dolphins at Delfinario

Children's Attractions

1 Cueva del Indio

This underground cavern in the Valle de San Vicente will delight children with its spooky, bat-ridden stalagmites and stalactites. The main thrill is a boat ride on an underground river that emerges into open air. Horseback rides are also offered. ◈ Map B2 • Carretera a San Vicente • (8) 79 6280 • Open 9am–5pm • Adm

2 Baseball

Older children will enjoy the buzz of an evening baseball game especially if familiar with the rules. It is a spectacle accompanied by lots of music and cheering, and the games often end late at night. ◈ Estadio Latinoamericano: Calle Consejero Arango & Pedro Pérez, Cerro, Havana; (7) 870 6526

3 Crocodile Farms

Kids can safely get close to Cuba's endemic crocodile in breeding farms found on the island. This monster grows to 16-ft (5-m) long. Younger crocodiles are kept apart. Some farms also breed the American crocodile (see p82).

A game of baseball

4 Cuban Schools

Most Cuban schools are small and intimate, and foreign children are almost always welcomed for brief visits. Local kids are usually curious to learn about foreign cultures. Make arrangements to visit in advance.

Kids dressed in school uniforms

5 Dolphin Shows

Cuba has four marine theme parks where trained bottlenose dolphins perform for visitors' amusement. ◈ Delfinario: Map F2; Carretera Las Morlas, km 11.5, Varadero; (45) 66 8031; open 9am-5pm; adm

6 Horse-Drawn Carriages

Enjoy the sights of Habana Vieja or Varadero on horse-drawn carriages as they clip-clop through cobbled streets. ◈ Horse-drawn Carriages: Map F2 • Parque Josone, Avenida 1ra, Varadero

7 Valle de la Prehistoria, Santiago de Cuba

Huge Tyrannosaurus rex occupy this prehistoric theme park, featuring life-size concrete reptiles. A natural science museum has informative displays on local wildlife (see p110).

8 Parque Histórico-Militar Morro-Cabaña, Havana

This ancient castle with clifftop battlements comes alive at dusk, with a daily ceremony which features real-life soldiers get dressed in the costumes of Independence soldiers, and march into the castle to fire a cannon. There is also a fine collection of blunderbusses, muskets, swords, and other yesteryear armaments (see p9).

9 Steam Train Rides

Cuba still has more than 100 steam trains puffing away. Though most of the trains are used to haul sugarcane, some have been spruced up for sightseeing trips. In Trinidad, kids can whistle down the tracks of the Valle de los Ingenios (see p97) on a 1907 "choo-choo," or ride around Havana's Parque Lenin in an antique train.

10 Fun Fairs

Nearly every town in Cuba has a parque de diversiones (a fun park) with carousels and other rides. The Todo en Uno fair in Varadero has modern rides that include carros locos (bumper cars) and carousel rides. Havana's main fun park is in Parque Lenin. 🕲 Todo en Uno: Map F2 • Autopista Sur & Calle 54, Varadero • Open 6–11pm Tue–Thu, 11am–11pm Fri–Sun • Adm

Tourist steam-engine trains

Top 10 Activities for Children in Havana

1 Acuario Nacional
The sea lion and dolphin show enthralls crowds at the National Aquarium.

2 Cañonazo
Soldiers fire a cannon at 9pm nightly from this fortress. 🕲 Map X1

3 Clowns
Payasos (clowns) on stilts wander the streets entertaining children.

4 Horseback Rides
Kids can mount horses in Parque Lenin, or clip-clop around Parque Luz y Caballero, one block north of Plaza de la Catedral.

5 Parque Zoológico Nacional
The national zoo's main draw is its African wildlife safari and drive-through lion's pit. 🕲 Capdevilla, km 3.5, Rancho Boyeros • (7) 644 7613

6 Playas del Este
These family-friendly beaches outside Havana have warm waters (see p48).

7 Prado
A great place to interact with Cuban children who enjoy roller-skating.

8 Teatro Guiñol
This theater in Vedado has comedy and marioneta (puppet) shows. 🕲 Map U1 • Calle M & 17 • (7) 832 6262

9 Teatro para niños Cinecito
Cinema showing cartoons with Spanish subtitles. 🕲 Map W2 • Calle San Rafael & Consulado • (7) 863 8051

10 Trompoloco Circus
Clowns and acrobats perform beneath a huge circus tent. 🕲 Calle 112, Playa • (7) 206 5641

Left **A panoramic view of Las Terrazas in Pinar del Rio province** Right **Topes de Collantes**

Nature Trails

1 Las Terrazas

This mountain resort is Cuba's premier ecotourism destination, with trails, waterfalls, mineral springs, and coffee plantations surrounded by forest. The Moka Hotel *(see p132)* provides decent lodgings *(see p12)*.

2 Valle de Viñales

Surrounded by *mogotes*, Valle de Viñales has the most dramatic scenery in Cuba. Among its best trails is one that ascends the east flank of the Sierra de Viñales to the Comunidad de Aquáticos, a community that ritualizes the powers of water. S *Map B2*

3 Península de Guanahacabibes

At the far western tip of Cuba, this slender peninsula is covered with a rare expanse of tropical dry forest – a protected habitat for *jutías*, *jabalís*, and over 170 bird species. For birding and visits to caves, there are the Cueva de las Perlas and Sendero del Bosque al Mar trails. S *Map A3 • Estación Ecológica: La Bajada, Sandino (48) 75 0366*

A horseback rider at Finca La Belén

4 Topes de Collantes

This spa-resort complex on the southeast flank of the Sierra del Escambray *(see p89)* makes a perfect base for exploring the steep trails through scented pine forests, and waterfalls crashing into crystal-clear pools. The Parque Codina trail leads to an ancient coffee estate. Squawking parrots tear through the treetops and the *tocororo* – Cuba's national bird *(see p50)* – can also often be spotted.

5 Finca La Belén

A walk or horseback ride from this working farm, which exhibits zebra and various exotic cattle, leads through semideciduous woodland and montane forests that help protect the different types of endemic plants including a rare cactus species. Birders will have a field day spotting parrots and colorful avian fauna. S *Map L4 • 27 miles (43 km) SE of Camagüey • (32) 86 4349 • Adm: for horseback rides and guided bird tours*

The dramatic Valle de Viñales

Parque Nacional Desembarco del Granma

This dry and dusty park is the starting point for several recommended trails that take you through a cactus-studded dry tropical forest. Bird-watching is a big draw here, and manatees are sometimes seen in mangrove lagoons. The El Guafe trail leads to a large cave full of fanciful limestone formations *(see p111)*.

The distinctive El Yunque mountain

Pinares de Mayarí

The Pinares de Mayarí are virtually impossible to reach except by four-wheel drive or on an organized tour. This large area of montane wilderness is a popular base for guided hikes, like the one to the Salto el Guayabo waterfall *(see p112)*. A mountain resort that was created for the reigning Communist Party elite is now open to tourists.
◎ Map P5 • 12 miles (19 km) S of Mayarí, Holguín province • (24) 50 3308 • Gaviota@gaviota.cu

Orchid at Parque Nacional Alejandro Humboldt

Pico Turquino

Cuba's highest mountain can be ascended from either north or south sides, the most popular starting point being Santo Domingo. At least two days are required, and guides are compulsory for the arduous climb. You will need to pre-arrange a second set of guides if you plan to traverse the mountain. ◎ Map N6 • Departure 8am • Adm: permit including guides • Book visit at the Ecotur office, Hotel Sierra Maestra: Carretera Central, km 1.5, Bayamo; (23) 42 4875

Parque Nacional Alejandro Humboldt

Protecting the richest flora and fauna in Cuba, most of this wilderness is covered with dense rain forest and mangroves along the shore. The various trails range from easy walks to challenging climbs to the Balcón de Iberia waterfall *(see p112)*.

El Yunque

The unique flat-topped El Yunque mountain can be accessed by trail from Baracoa for a climb accompanied by a compulsory guide. The rewards are the staggering panoramic view and a chance to spot exotic birds *(see p27)*.

Left **Playas del Este** Right **Playa Flamingo**

🔟 Beach Resorts

Cuba's Top 10

1 Playas del Este
Meandering for several miles east of Havana, this long sweeping stretch of beaches is popular with the capital's citizens as a weekend hangout. Pounding surf and a powerful undertow can be a deterrent to swimmers. The prettiest sections are Playa Santa María and Playa El Mégano, with gorgeous white sands and plenty of beach facilities. ◈ Map H5

2 Cayo Levisa
This small island, ringed by white sands, an offshore coral reef, and mangroves, is renowned for its superb scuba diving. Coconut trees sway enticingly over a small resort, totally rebuilt since the Hurricane Wilma swept it off the map in 2005. ◈ Map C2

3 Playa Sirena, Cayo Largo
Only a few miles from the all-inclusive hotels of Cayo Largo (see p81), is Playa Sirena with its broad swathe of pure white sand

and thatched restaurants. The waters are an alluring blue and perfect for watersports, but the walk-in is steep and not suitable for children. Access to Cayo Largo is no longer restricted to only tourists, and many visitors lie naked on the sands. ◈ Map E4

4 Playa Mayor, Varadero
Lined with hotels for almost its entire length, this long stretch of silvery sand is the most well developed beach in Cuba. Still, there is enough space for everyone, and the peacock-blue waters are warm and inviting. However, tourist interactions with Cubans are restrained by a heavy police presence. ◈ Map F1

5 Playa Ancón
Shaded by Australian pine, this white-sand beach lying along the Ancón Peninsula is within a 20-minute drive of Trinidad (see p16). The Cuban government is in the process of gradually developing it as a tourist resort and now three all-inclusive hotels and a diving school are located here. The Caribbean seas offer superb snorkeling and diving, but swimmers need to be careful of the microscopic sea lice that sometimes infest the waters and can result in the occurrence of flu-like infections (see p17).

Mangroves on the shores of Cayo Levisa

6 Playa Periquillo, Cayo Santa María

A long *pedraplén* (causeway) arcs across a shallow lagoon to reach the low-lying Playa Periquillo bay. The beach is a slender scimitar with warm waters. The shallows offer excellent bonefishing, while coral reefs and a wreckage are perfect for diving enthusiasts. ✎ *Map J1*

An elevated view of Playa Ancón

7 Playa Flamingo, Cayo Coco

One of the most beautiful beaches in the country, Playa Flamingo boasts white sand and turquoise waters protected by an offshore coral reef. With half a dozen large, beach-front hotels, the facilities here continue to expand as new hotels are added. However, there is plenty of wilderness as well. Wildlife, including the flamingos from whom the beach gets its name, parade around the inshore lagoons *(see p18)*.

8 Playa Pilar, Cayo Guillermo

Brushed by near constant breezes, the white sands of this beach are swept into dunes overlooking pristine reef-protected ocean waters where you can wade knee-deep for 400 yards (366 m). Water birds can be found frolicking in the lagoons and mangroves alongside hungry mosquitoes. ✎ *Map K1*

9 Playa Esmeralda, Guardalavaca

Lying on the indented Atlantic coastline of Holguín province, Emerald Beach is truly a jewel. When you tire of the sands, wander along the ecological trails that lead through a mangrove and dry forest preserve, or take in the local sights. ✎ *Map K1*

10 Playa Siboney

The pebbly gray sand here may not be the finest in Cuba, but the setting is lovely. Playa Siboney is one of few places where you can interact with locals and enjoy the rhythm of the salsa with them. Accommodation is offered in Caribbean wooden homes. ✎ *Map P6*

Left **Flamingos taking off** Right **Cuban crocodile**

Top 10 Animals and Birds

1 Cuban Crocodile
Up to 16 ft (5 m) in length, the Cuban crocodile is endemic to the island and is far more aggressive than its cousin, the American crocodile, which is also found here. Despite being hunted to near extinction, the population has recovered thanks to a breeding program introduced by Fidel Castro.

2 Solenodon
You are unlikely to see one of these long-nosed, ant-eating mammals in the wild, as they are shy and nocturnal. Resembling a giant shrew, the solenodon is an endangered species, as it is easy prey for dogs and mongooses. A few can be seen in captivity.

3 Polymite
These snails are remarkable for their colorful shells, whorled in patterns that are unique to each individual snail. The shells of these multicolored mollusks can range from simple black-and-white spirals to blazing stripes of orange, yellow, and maroon. Cuba's polymite population has plummeted in recent years.

Polymite

4 Tocororo
This pigeon-sized, forest-dwelling bird is a member of the trogon family. The tocororo is Cuba's national bird because its blue, white, and red plumage corresponds to the colors of the nation's flag. It has a serrated bill, concave-tipped tail, and is common throughout the island.

The tocororo

5 Flamingo
Standing atop legs that resemble carnation stalks this pink bird is the most attractive of Cuba's many estuary birds. Large flocks of flamingos inhabit the salt-water lagoons of Zapata. They primarily eat insect larvae, which contain a substance that gives them their bright color.

6 Hutia
A shy mammal, the endemic hutia looks like an overgrown guinea pig. This rabbit-sized herbivore is endangered by deforestation, illegal hunting, and predators. It inhabits many of the wilderness regions of Cuba, but is most likely to be seen in captivity. Many Cubans breed hutias for food.

7 Zunzuncito
The tiny Cuban hummingbird is so small, it is often mistaken for a bee; earning it the nickname "bee hummer." In fact, at only one inch (2.5 cm) long, it

A pair of iguanas

is the world's smallest bird. Nonetheless, this feisty bantam defends its territory aggressively and has even been seen attacking vultures.

8 Iguana
Resembling a small dragon, this leathery reptile inhabits offshore cays and feasts on leaves, fruit, and occasionally insects. It basks in the sun to become active, but seeks refuge from the mid-afternoon heat in cool burrows.

9 Jabalí
The Cuban wild boar is known for its aggressive nature when threatened. Covered in thick bristles, it is common to lowland wilderness areas. The *jabalí* is hunted for sport – its meat is a local delicacy.

10 Cuban Parrot
The *cotorra*, or parrot, an inhabitant of dry forests, was once found throughout Cuba. Now threatened, it is most easily seen in the Zapata swamps, on Isla de la Juventud, and in Parque Alejandro Von Humboldt. It performs noisy mating displays during the onset of the wet season.

The *cotorra*

Top 10 Cuban Trees and Flowers

1 Royal Palm
Cuba's silver-sheathed national tree is a beautiful palm with feather-like fronds.

2 Mangrove
Five species of mangroves grow along Cuba's shores, rising from the waters on a tangle of interlocking stilts.

3 Ceiba
With a huge limbless trunk topped by wide-spreading boughs, this tree is considered sacred by believers of *santería*.

4 Jagüey
Seeding atop host trees, this species drops roots to the ground and envelopes and chokes its host.

5 Sea Grape
This hardy shrub grows along shores and issues broad, circular leaves and bunches of grape-like fruit.

6 Orchid
Hundreds of orchid species grow in Cuba from the plains to the mountains.

7 Creolean Pine
Native to the Caribbean, this species is found above about 5,000 ft (1,524 m).

8 Bougainvillea
Brightening many towns, the spectacular pink, purple, and bright red "flowers" of this shrub are, in fact, leaves surrounding tiny petals.

9 Flamboyán
Flowering flame-red, this wide-spreading tree emblazons the country in spring and summer.

10 Cork Palm
The endangered cork palm grows only in remote areas of the Cordillera de Guaniguanico (see p80).

Left **Día de los Trabajadores parade** Right **Venue for Festival de Nuevo Cine Latinoamericano**

🔟 Festivals and Holidays

1 Jan 1, Liberation Day
New Year's Day in Cuba is celebrated as the day that dictator Fulgencio Batista *(see p41)* was toppled. Officially known as the "Anniversary of the Triumph of the Revolution," the event is commemorated with nationwide musical concerts.

2 Jan 28, José Martí's Birthday
Cubans celebrate the birth of their national hero *(see p31)* with events including readings of Martí's poetry and concerts. Kids are integral to the celebrations.

3 Apr 19, Victoria de Playa Girón
The plaza and museum behind the beach at Playa Girón is the setting for speeches, a wreath-laying ceremony and festivities to celebrate the "first defeat of imperialism in the Americas." The holiday also honors the Cuban victory in the Bay of Pigs invasion *(see p31)*.

4 May 1, Día de los Trabajadores
As many as half a million communists march through Plaza de la Revolución *(see p11)* while Cuba's leaders look on. Rallies full of patriotic songs are held throughout the island as Cubans proclaim their dedication to socialism and the Revolution.

5 Jul 26, National Revolution Day
A celebration of the launch of the Revolution of 1953 *(see p33)* is held in a different city each year. Attendees dress in black and red T-shirts – the colors of Castro's M-7-26 revolutionary movement – and listen to speeches by Communist leaders.

6 July, Carnaval
Many major cities organize some sort of street carnival in July featuring live music and dancing showgirls. The biggest event is in Santiago de Cuba, where carnival season climaxes with a parade of bands along Avenida Jesús Menéndez. 🔊 *Map P6*

7 Oct 8, Anniversary of Che Guevara's death
Santa Clara's Plaza de la Revolución and the Monumento del Che *(see p32)* are the setting for a wreath-laying ceremony in the presence of key political leaders.

Musicians at the Carnaval

To find out more on Cuba's history **See pp30–31**

Oct 28, Memorial to Camilo Cienfuegos

Schoolchildren in Havana march to the Malecón (see p11) to throw "a flower for Camilo" into the sea on the anniversary of the death of Cienfuegos (see p35). This revolutionary commander died in 1959 in a mysterious plane crash. There is also a parade to the sea at the Museo de Camilo Cienfuegos in Jaguajay, Sancti Spíritus province (see p97).

Nov, Festival de Ballet

For 10 days in November, Havana's Gran Teatro (see p69) plays host to brilliant ballet performances featuring leading international dancers and ballet corps. Hosted by the Ballet National de Cuba, the festival is one of the major events in the bi-annual cultural calendar.

Dec, Festival de Nuevo Cine Latinoamericano

Cubans are inveterate movie-goers and the highlight of their year is the Havana Film Festival, which screens a variety of art-house films and documentaries from around the world, as well as off-beat works from some of Cuba's own first-rate directors.

Festival de Ballet

Top 10 Local Festivals

1 Holguín (Jan), Semana de Cultura Holguinera
The town comes alive with a medley of cultural activities.

2 Camagüey (Feb), Jornadas de la Cultura Camagüeyana
This city celebrates its founding with much fanfare.

3 Trinidad (Easter), El Recorrido del Vía Cruce
Catholic devotees follow the ancient "way of the cross."

4 Cienfuegos (Aug), Festival Internacional Benny Moré
Celebrated every other year to honor Benny Moré (see p43).

5 Santiago de Cuba (Aug), Festival de Pregón
Citizens converge on Parque Céspedes to recite traditional songs and verses.

6 Las Tunas (Jun), Jornada Cucalambeana
Singers compete in décimas – 10-syllable rhyming verses – to honor this composer.

7 Guantánamo (Dec), Festival del Changüí
An excuse to party as son groups perform (see p43).

8 Trinidad (Dec), Fiestas Navideñas
The journey of Mary and Joseph is re-created.

9 Rincón (Dec 17), Procesión de los Milagros
The orisha San Lázaro is honored in this pilgrimage.

10 Remedios (24–29 Dec), Parrandas
Two sides of town duel in a firework contest (see p88).

Left **Baseball fans gathered at Parque Central** Right **Sunbathers at Playas del Este near Havana**

Places to Meet the Locals

1 Parque Central, Havana
Havana has many plazas, but this tree-shaded park on the edge of Old Havana is the liveliest. Baseball fans gather here to argue the finer points of the game. With plenty of benches, it is a tremendous place to watch the flurry of activity. Expect to have *jineteros* (hustlers) approach you to tout their wares or services *(see p121)*.

2 The Malecón, Havana
The cooling breezes of the capital's seafront boulevard attracts *habaneros* (Havana locals) of all ages, who socialize with guitars and bottles of rum. On hot days families bathe in the *balnearios* cut into the limestone rock. Take care to watch your step – the pavement is crumbling and waves often crash over the seawall *(see p11)*.

3 Calle Obispo, Havana
This pedestrian-only shopping street has plenty of intriguing shops, bars, cafés, and ice-cream stores, where many private art galleries display their works. Pickpockets are on the prowl, so guard your belongings *(see p74)*.

4 Baseball Games
Watching a Cuban baseball game is as much a social experience as a sporting one. The crowds are passionate but friendly, and the game is interspersed with chatting and drinking. You will make new friends here, even if you support the "other" team.

5 Playas del Este
On weekends, families flee Havana for a day at the beach. Singles and tourists interact toward the west end, despite a disapproving police presence. Many families prefer the beach around Guanabo *(see p48)*.

6 Casas de la Trova
When bitten by the dancing bug, head to a Casa de la Trova. Every town has one of these traditional music houses, where Cuban singles as well as couples have a great time dancing to timeless *sons* and *boleros*.

7 Cumbanchas
Few Cubans have money for discos, so they spark up their own song and dance at street parties where anyone can join in. Contribute a bottle of rum, the

The seafront along Havana's Malecón

Shoppers at Calle Obispo, Havana

drink of choice, as courtesy. Cubans are not shy, and even if you arrive with a partner, expect to be asked to dance.

Cabarets

Cuban couples adore these traditional and sexy revues featuring scantily clad dancers and great salsa music. There is at least one cabaret in every major town, and even in some remote villages. Most couples linger for the discos that typically follow the show. Tables are usually shared – everyone chips in for a bottle of rum and cola.

Mercados Agropecuarios

The farmers' markets are packed with Cubans shopping for fresh produce, while others enjoy the local gossip. Every town has at least one "agro." Even if you are not planning to buy, the atmosphere makes a visit worthwhile.

Casas de la Cultura

These cultural centers found in every town draw a cross-section of society, who come to enjoy activities such as literary readings and traditional music. The atmosphere is informal and these are a great place to make new friends and perhaps learn a few dance moves.

Top 10 Customs and Beliefs

1 Politeness
Old-fashioned courtesy, such as saying "Thank you!" and "Please!", is very important to Cuban people.

2 Dress
Even impoverished Cubans dress as well as their budget will allow. Scruffiness is not appreciated.

3 Santería
More than half the Cuban population are followers of this Afro-Cuban religion *(see pp38–9)*

4 Racial Harmony
Cuba is an ethnically diverse society and the degree of racial harmony on the island is profound.

5 Equality
The concept of equality for all on every level is a concept Cubans hold close to their hearts.

6 Take it easy
Hurrying is uncommon in Cuba where foreigners who expect things to happen quickly can be disappointed.

7 Greetings
Cubans greet everyone upon entering a room. People refer to each other as *compañero* (companion).

8 Machismo
This is totally ingrained among most men – even married men flirt openly.

9 "The New Man"
Che Guevara dreamed of creating a society where people are motivated by altruism, a key tenet of the Revolution.

10 Chistes (Jokes)
A great sense of humor helps many Cubans deal with the hardships of daily life – the subject of most *chistes*.

Cuba's Top 10

Left **Corvina al Ajillo** Right **Cerdo Asado**

TOP 10 Cuban Dishes

1 Moros y Cristianos
The base of *comida criolla* (traditional Cuban fare), this dish comprises white rice cooked with black beans and is served as an accompaniment to meat and seafood meals. It is known as *congrí* when cooked with red beans and *congrí oriental* when the red and black beans are mixed.

2 Ropa Vieja
The "old rope" is a combination of boiled rice, black beans, fried plantain, and shredded beef marinated in red wine or rum, seasoned with onions, peppers, oregano, and cumin.

Ropa Vieja

3 Cerdo Asado
Pork is roasted in an open oven or on a spit, and is served whole on skewers. *Cerdo Asado*

Ajiaco

is usually served with rice and black beans accompanied by fried plantain.

4 Corvina al Ajillo
This simple and delicate seabass dish is typically combined with slices of lime and regular vegetables such as carrots. Either mashed potatoes or *moros y cristianos* are served on the side.

5 Ajiaco
This minestrone-style vegetable stew is made with *malanga*, turnips, corn and yucca, plus a variety of meats, including pork and chicken. It is seasoned with oregano and other herbs.

6 Bistec Uruguayo
"Uruguayan beef," a staple found on many restaurant menus, is a steak stuffed with ham and cheese. It is usually accompanied by a side salad of boiled vegetables, mashed potatoes or rice, and beans. Fish and chicken are often used instead of beef.

7 Pollo Montuno
A traditional country recipe, this dish is a chicken casserole simmered with onions, ginger, and cloves of garlic, sweetened with sugarcane syrup, wine, or even rum, and seasoned with

Chicken and fish are often used as substitutes for beef, which is a rarity found in only a few state-run restaurants.

Flan de huevos

parsley and basil. It is served with a bowl of steamed or boiled *malanga*, yams, and potatoes, accompanied by white rice.

8 Potaje
Black beans are slow-cooked with garlic, onions, pepper, oregano, and other herbs to produce this delicious, thick soup. Sometimes pieces of pork or chicken are added. A bowl of plain white rice is usually the sole accompaniment.

9 Enchilada de Langosta
Lobster is typically boiled, then cooked in a sauce of tomatoes and spiced with peppers and other seasonings. Shrimp is often used as a substitute for lobster. It is usually served with rice and a salad of lettuce and boiled vegetables.

10 Flan
Cuba's most popular dessert, apart from ice cream, this custard is found on most menus. It closely resembles *crème brûlée* and is made from eggs and milk. It is almost always served with a sugary syrup and sometimes the custard is served caramelized.

Top 10 Drinks

1 Mojito
This world-famous Cuban drink is made of white rum with mint leaves, sugar, and a dash of soda water.

2 Cuba Libre
Dark rum with cola and natural lime juice served with plenty of ice in a tall glass, garnished with a lime.

3 Cristal
A light, lager-style beer, usually served chilled. It has a milder taste than the more full-bodied Bucanero beer.

4 Rum
Younger "white" rums are used for most cocktails, while aged rums – *añejos* – are typically drunk straight.

5 Daiquirí
White rum blended with sugar, lime juice, and crushed ice and served in a broad glass decorated with a maraschino cherry.

6 Fruit Juices
Many tropical fruits are packaged as fresh juices, including *guayaba* (guava), grapefruit, and orange.

7 Batidos
Water or milk is blended with ice and fresh fruit, such as mango and papaya to make a refreshing shake.

8 Refrescos
An infinite variety of tropical fruit-flavored, water-based, sweetened drinks.

9 Pru
Made from various herbs and roots, this medicinal drink is served in the eastern provinces of Cuba.

10 Chorote
Strongly flavored chocolate drink of Baracoa, thickened with cornstarch and sweetened with sugar.

Left *Guayaberas* Center **Artisan painting traditional Spanish fan** Right **Souvenirs made of seeds**

🔟 Things to Buy

1 Guayaberas
This Cuban cotton shirt worn by men is ideal for beating the heat. It features a straight hem and is worn draped outside the trousers. Either long- or short-sleeved, the shirts usually have four buttoned pockets and are embroidered with twin, vertical stripes down the front.

2 Che Guevara T-shirts
Almost every Cuban souvenir store and flea market sells cotton T-shirts for men, women, and children. The most common image is the iconic photo of Che Guevara in his trademark black beret with the five-point revolutionary star.

Che Guevara T-shirt

3 Wood Carvings

Carved wooden statues are a staple of craft markets found all over Cuba. The most common items, which make good gifts, are exaggeratedly slender nude female figures made of mahogany, ebony, and *lignum vitae*. Bowls and plates are also available as are chess sets and humidors, often in colorful combinations of different types of hardwoods.

African-style figure

4 Fans
Traditional, handmade, and prettily painted Spanish fans or *abanicos* make a great gift. The fans are hand-painted in an age-old tradition. Gift shops throughout Cuba also sell them.

5 Papier Mâché Cars
Cuban artisans are skilled at making papier mâché items, and pre-revolutionary American automobiles are a popular theme. These can be incredibly lifelike, or eccentric, smile-inducing distortions. Look for papier mâché *muñequitas* (dolls) of the *orishas* and figures of baseball players as well as cigar-smoking *mulattas* (Santeria deities).

6 Music CDs
CDs and cassette tapes of everything from *son* to *salsa* are widely available in *casas de la trova, (see p54)*, souvenir stores, and shops run by the state-owned recording entity, EGREM. Musicians who perform at restaurants and other such venues often offer recordings of their music for sale.

7 Coffee
Some of the best mountain-grown beans in the Caribbean are sold in vacuum-sealed packages at reasonable prices. Many shops sell an export-quality brand called Cubanita.

All of these goods are widely available at souvenir stores and flea markets throughout Cuba.

8 Cuban Art

Although much of Cuban art is kitsch, mass-produced, and repetitious, the nation's many artists also produce some of the most visually exciting works in the Caribbean. Colorful re-creations of typical street scenes featuring old American auto-mobiles or ox-drawn carts are irresistible, but also look for more profound works by contemporary masters. The former are sold at street markets nation-wide; the latter are represented at quality state-run galleries.

9 Jewelry

Scour the street markets for creative avant-garde pieces made from recycled cutlery. Black coral finds its way into contemporary silver, and sometimes into gold jewelry sold at state-run *joyerías* (jewelry stores) in Havana. Black coral looks very pretty when set in jewelry, but bear in mind that it is a threatened species.

10 Lace

Much of Cuba's lovely, traditional lace embroidery is from Trinidad, the center of homespun production. Look for exquisite tablecloths, anti-macassars, blouses, as well as pretty, crocheted bikinis.

Colorful local paintings

Top 10 Rums and Cigars

1 Havana Club Gran Reserva
Aged for 15 years, this is the finest of all Cuban rums, with a texture and flavor like a superb cognac.

2 Ron Matusalem Añejo
Elegant rum aged in barrels for 10 years, three years longer than most *añejos*.

3 Cohiba Siglo
Large, flawless cigar loaded with flavor.

4 Vega Robaina
Hand-rolled cigars using choice filler and Cuba's finest wrapper leaves.

5 Varadero Oro
Aged for five years, this dark golden rum is smooth, sweet, and has distinctive caramel flavors.

6 Partagás Series D
A full-bodied cigar with an intense, earthy flavor, this Robusto is the standard-bearer of the Partagás brand.

7 Montecristo Figurados No. 2
This extremely rare, perfectly balanced, distinctly flavored, torpedo-shaped cigar is much sought after by connoisseurs.

8 Ron Santiago 45 Aniversario
Limited edition, well-aged rum with hints of honey and walnuts – one of Cuba's finest.

9 Romeo y Julieta Churchill
This long, large, full-bodied smoke is considered the finest cigar produced by the Romeo y Julieta factory.

10 Trinidad Fundadores
A classic considered perhaps the finest of Cuban cigars, Fidel Castro presents these to visiting dignitaries.

Left **A classic American car** Right **Local baseball game**

10 American Legacies

1 American Autos
Time seems to have stood still for five decades on Cuban roads, where one in every eight cars dates back to before the Revolution *(see p31)*. Most are American classics from the 1950s – including models that vanished from US roads years ago.

Dancers at the Tropicana in the 1940s

2 Tropicana
A fixture of Havana's night scene since opening on New Year's Eve in 1939, this Las Vegas-style cabaret has more than 200 performers, including statuesque showgirls and amazing gymnasts *(see p69)*.

3 Baseball
Americans introduced baseball to Cuba in the mid-19th century. Today, the island produces some of the finest players. Cuban teams regularly defeat US teams at the Olympics.

4 Art Deco
Cuban cities are graced with Art Deco buildings that date back to the 1930s and the heyday of Hollywood movies. The finest are the cinemas, often with rounded architectural elements and horizontal banding. These designs exemplify the architects' desire to imbue local buildings with slick, streamlined forms, reflecting the great age of transport.

5 US Naval Base
When the US government wrote Cuba's Constitution in 1902 *(see p30)*, it included a clause – the Platt Amendment – granting itself a perpetual lease of Guantánamo Bay. The naval base is a bone of contention today in American/Cuban relations. The US government writes a check every year for the annual lease, but Fidel Castro *(see pp34–5)* refuses to cash it. ◈ *Map Q6*

6 Hotel Nacional
Symbolic of Havana's decadent pre-revolutionary heyday, this hotel *(see p11)* was built in 1930 in Spanish Neo-Classical style and was closely associated with the Mafia. Actor Marlon Brando and supermodel Naomi Campbell feature in the hotel's celebrity guest list *(see p11)*.

Spanish Neo-Classical style Hotel Nacional

Socializing on the Malecón

Malecón
Havana's seafront boulevard was laid out in 1902 by US Army General Leonard Woods. It took another 50 years for the six-lane causeway to be extended to the Río Almendares. Now officially known as Avenida Antonio Maceo, it is lined with late 19th-century buildings and high-rise hotels (see p11).

Hotel Habana Libre
This national monument opened in March 1958 as the Havana Hilton. Built in Modernist style with 630 rooms, it was the largest and tallest hotel in Latin America, and featured a casino and supper club. The hotel also once served as Fidel Castro's headquarters (see p69).

Ernest Hemingway
The famous US author first came to Cuba in 1932 to fish for marlin. He fell in love with the island and it was here that he wrote For Whom the Bell Tolls. In 1940 he bought Finca Vigía (see p36) outside Havana, making it his home for 20 years.

Steam Trains
Creaking engines towing carriages piled high with sugar-cane are a common sight in Cuba, which has more than 100 working steam trains – more than any other country except China. Most were made in Philadelphia in the 1920s.

Top 10 American Autos

1 1955 Chevrolet Bel-Air
This was a perfectly proportioned 1950s icon.

2 1958 Edsel Corsair
Launched in 1958, the Edsel Corsair's styling drew more laughs than praise. Production of the flamboyant folly ended the following year.

3 1959 Cadillac Eldorado
Reflecting the pinnacle of exorbitant late-1950s styling, this rocket-like car was inspired by the space race.

4 1951 Chevrolet Styline
This Chevy was the most commonly seen classic car in Cuba.

5 1950 Studebaker Champion
Its unmistakable bullet-nose design proved to be popular with Cubans.

6 1951 Kaiser Traveler
Ahead of its time, this excellent car had many safety features that the US government would later mandate.

7 1951 Pontiac Chieftain
This car had a likeness of a Native American chieftain on its hood, which lit up when the headlights were on.

8 1953 Buick Super
Famed for its "grinning tooth" grill, this car's Dyna-flow three-speed transmission was nicknamed "Dynaslush" for its slow responsiveness.

9 1951 Hudson Hornet
Its ground-hugging profile and power made it a winner in stock-car racing.

10 1952 Oldsmobile Super 88
This behemoth had power steering and a lightweight body that promised "one finger" parking.

AROUND
CUBA

CUBA'S TOP 10

[]

Left **Interior of Iglesia San Francisco** Right **Entrance to the Museo Nacional de Belles Artes**

Havana

FROM THE COLONIAL SPLENDOR OF HABANA VIEJA *(Old Havana)* to the faded early 20th-century grandeur of Vedado, central Havana is replete with castles, palaces, mansions, and cathedrals. Centered on four colonial plazas, much of Habana Vieja has been restored and teems with atmospheric hotels, top-notch restaurants, trendy boutiques, and lively bars. Farther afield, Vedado is laid out on an easily navigated grid of tree-shaded streets lined with once resplendent mansions. The main attractions are the amazing university and cemetery, and the Plaza de la Revolución, the setting for many of the impressive political marches past and present. Vedado's nightclubs from its 1950s heyday still sizzle, and the high-rise hotels of the same era are a popular draw even today.

Sights

1. Catedral de San Cristóbal
2. Plaza de Armas
3. Plaza Vieja
4. Iglesia y Convento San Francisco
5. Calle Mercaderes
6. Museo Nacional de Bellas Artes
7. Museo de la Revolución
8. Capitolio
9. Parque Central
10. Plaza de la Revolución

Capitolio

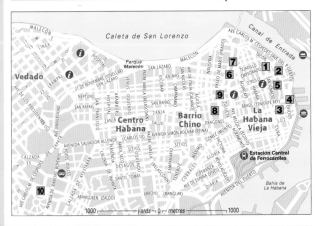

Preceding pages **View of a beach at Varadero**

Plaza Vieja

1 Catedral de La Habana

Havana's charming cathedral (1777), officially known as the Catedral de la Virgen María de la Concepción Inmaculada, has an exquisite Baroque façade supported by pilasters and asymmetrical bell towers. The relatively austere altar has fading frescoes by Giuseppe Perovani. Of the eight side chapels, the largest is Capella Sagracio, which contains tiny houses used as ex-votos. The plaza is surrounded by colonial mansions and enlivened by pretty *mulattas* dressed in colorful colonial costumes *(see p8)*.

2 Plaza de Armas

This cobbled plaza *(see p8)*, laid out in the 1600s as the administrative center of Cuba, is named for the military exercises that took place here. It is surrounded by notable buildings, such as the Castillo de la Real Fuerza *(see p37)*, the temple-like Neo-Classical El Templete, and the Palacio de Los Capitanes Generales – a former governor's palace that houses Museo de la Ciudad *(see p36)*. ❧ *Map X4*
• *El Templete: open 9am–7pm; adm*

3 Plaza Vieja

Dating from 1559, this attractive plaza *(see p9)* consists of columned arcades. Interesting buildings spanning four centuries rise on each side of the square. The 18th-century Casa del Conde de Jaruco hosts art exhibitions, while the Museo de Naipes exhibits a collection of playing cards. On the southeast corner, the Art Nouveau Palacio Vienna Hotel is being resurrected.
❧ *Map X5 • Casa del Conde Jaruco: Calle Muralla 107; (7) 862 2633; open 10am–5pm Mon–Sat • Museo de Naipes: (7) 860 1534; adm*

4 Iglesia y Convento San Francisco

The grandiose Basílica Menor de San Francisco de Asís ceased to be used for worship following British occupation in 1762. Today it hosts music concerts. The adjoining cloisters of the former convent house is a museum of religious art. An open crypt displays bodies of important colonial citizens *(see p9)*.

Castillo de la Real Fuerza, Plaza de Armas

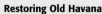

Calle Mercaderes
5 This cobbled street *(see p9)* is lined with colonial mansions housing tiny museums, boutiques, and other fascinating places. The three blocks might take a full morning to explore, with requisite stops at the Museo de Asia, Museo del Tabaco, and Maqueta de La Habana – a fabulous scale-model of Habana Vieja. Break your stroll at Mesón de la Flota, a *bodega* hosting live flamenco. Ⓢ *Map X1 • Museo de Asia: Calle Mercaderes 111, Habana Vieja; (7) 863 9740; open Tue–Sat 9am–5pm, Sun 9am–1pm • Museo del Tabaco: Calle Mercaderes 120, Habana Vieja; (7) 861 5795; open Tue–Sat 10am–5pm, Sun 9am–1pm; adm • Maqueta de La Habana: Calle Mercaderes 114, Habana Vieja; (7) 866 4425; open 9:30am–6pm daily; adm*

The dome at the Museo de la Revolución

Museo Nacional de Bellas Artes
6 This world-class museum has two parts. An international section occupies the Renaissance-style Centro Asturiano, built in 1927, and boasts treasures from ancient Egypt, Greece, and Rome. There are also works by European and North American masters, which include Gainsborough, Goya, and Rubens. The Modernist Palace of Fine Arts, a separate building two blocks away, displays works by Cuban artists *(see p41)* from different periods *(see p9)*.

Museo de la Revolución
7 Housed in the former presidential palace once occupied by General Batista, this museum is a tribute to the Revolution *(see p31)*, from the guerrilla war to the current day. The ornate, domed building, built in 1920, is as fascinating as the collection, and includes the Salón de los Espejos, a hall lined with mirrors. At the rear is the Granma Memorial *(see p32)*, featuring the yacht *Granma* as well as aircrafts and vehicles used in the Bay of Pigs invasion *(see p31)*.

Capitolio
8 The nation's grandiose former congressional building was inaugurated in 1929 and incorporates Art Deco elements into a Neo-Classical design that closely resembles Washington D.C.'s Capitol. It has been restored and is open to the public. Visitors approach via a steep flight of

Ministerio del Interior, Plaza de la Revolución

Parque Central

stairs flanked by classical bronze figures. A huge Statue of the Republic stands at the entrance hall, which features a fake 25-carat diamond embedded in the floor. The cavernous Salón de los Pasos Perdidos (Hall of Lost Steps), named so for its unusual acoustics, leads to the grand Chamber of Deputies *(see p10)*.

Parque Central

9 An epicenter of social life in Havana, this palm-shaded square has a statue of José Martí *(see p31)* and is surrounded by monumental 19th- and 20th-century buildings. These include the Neo-Classical Hotel Plaza and the spectacular Baroque Gran Teatro de la Habana *(see p69)*, which has angels mounted on its corner towers *(see p10)*.

Plaza de la Revolución

10 The administrative and political center of Cuba since the early 1950s, the plaza was laid out and surrounded with Modernist and monumentalist government buildings. Huge political rallies are held here. The Memorial José Martí on the south side features a large granite monument of the national hero, plus an excellent museum topped by a Surrealist tower. A visage of Che Guevara adorns the façade of the Ministerio del Interior *(see p11)*.

Habana Vieja Walk

Morning

After breakfast, head to **Plaza de la Catedral** *(see p8)*, the most intimate of the city's colonial plazas. Peek inside the **Cathedral** and then stop for a drink at Ernest Hemingway's favorite haunt, **La Bodeguita del Medio** *(see p72)*. Take photos of the locals dressed in colonial dresses before strolling along Calle San Ignacio, which is full of art galleries. Then turn left on Calle O'Reilly and walk two blocks south to **Plaza de Armas** *(see p8)*. Move around the square in a clockwise direction, stopping to admire the **Castillo de la Real Fuerza** *(see p37)*. On the park's southeast corner, explore the **Palacio de los Capitanes Generales** *(see p8)*. Opposite, the **Museo de la Plata** *(see p36)* is worth perusal before exiting the square along Calle Oficios. Take your time to admire the 18th-century buildings here.

Afternoon

Stop for refreshments at **La Paella** *(see p72)*, a *bodega*-style restaurant on Calle Obrapia. Revived, continue south to visit the **Iglesia y Convento San Francisco** *(see p9)*. Then walk toward **Plaza Vieja** *(see p9)*, where highlights include the Museo de Naipes, which displays playing cards through the ages, and the Cámara Oscura, a rooftop optical reflection camera that offers a magnified view of life from the top of Havana. End your day with a satisfying meal at **Restaurante Santo Ángel** *(see p72)*, just north of Plaza Vieja.

Left **Malecón** Center **Bronze lion statue at Paseo de Martí** Right **Cementerio Colón**

TOP 10 Best of the Rest

1 Malecón
Connecting colonial Habana Vieja to Vedado, this seafront boulevard offers grand vistas and is a gathering spot for locals. It's a splendid walk, but beware of street hustlers. ⊗ *Map S1–W1*

2 Fundación Destilería Havana Club
The Havana Club Foundation educates visitors on rum production. Rums can be sampled at the bar. ⊗ *Map T3 • Calle San Pedro 262, Habana Vieja • (7) 861 8051 • Open 9am–5pm Mon–Fri, 9am–4pm Sat • Adm (includes guided tour and drink) • www.havanaclubfoundation.com*

3 Paseo de Martí
"Prado" is a tree-shaded promenade guarded by bronze lions. Here, children receive lessons alfresco as locals sit and chat (see p10).

4 Fábrica de Tabacos Partágas
This cigar factory dates back to 1845 and provides a fascinating glimpse into cigar-making. ⊗ *Map W2 • Calle Industria 520, Centro Habana • (7) 862 0086 • Open 9:00–11am, noon–2:30pm Mon–Fri • Adm for guided tours*

5 Universidad de La Habana
The city's university boasts Neo-Classical buildings, two museums, and a staircase that was the setting for several violent demonstrations in pre-revolutionary days (see p11).

6 Hotel Nacional
An imposing Neo-Classical monument, this 1930s-era hotel draws visitors with its lavish decor, various bars, and gardens. ⊗ *Map V1 • Calle O & 21 • (7) 836 3564*

7 Cementerio Colón
One of the world's most astounding cemeteries, this massive necropolis features tombs representing a pantheon of important figures. ⊗ *Map S3 • Av. Zapata & Calle 12, Vedado • (7) 830 4517 • Open 8am–5pm daily • Adm (extra charge for guided tours and cameras)*

8 Miramar
The most elegant part of Havana, Miramar's leafy avenues are lined with grandiose mansions. Many modern deluxe hotels are located here.

9 Parque Histórico-Militar Morro-Cabaña
This vast military complex comprises the El Morro castle and the Fortaleza de San Carlos de la Cabaña, the largest fortress in the Americas. ⊗ *Map X1 • Carretera de la Cabaña • (7) 862 4095 • Open 8am–8pm daily (El Morro); 10am–10pm (San Carlos de la Cabaña) • Adm*

10 Museo Ernest Hemingway
Hemingway's former home has been maintained exactly the way he left it upon leaving Cuba (see p36). ⊗ *Map V3 • Calle Vigía, San Francisco de Paula • (7) 691 0809 • Open 9am–4:30pm Wed–Sun • Adm • mushem@cubarte.cult.cu*

Left **Steps of the Capitolio** Center **Façade of Edificio Bacardí** Right **Catedral de La Habana**

🔟 Architectural Gems

Capitolio
1 This grandiose congressional building is topped by a dome. Its highlight is the sumptuous Salón de los Pasos Perdidos – a hall with marble floor and gilded lamps *(see p66)*.

Catedral de La Habana
2 The Baroque façade of this 18th-century church is adorned with pilasters and spanned by asymmetrical bell towers, each thinner than the next *(see p8)*.

Edificio Bacardí
3 A stunning example of Art Deco, this soaring, multi-tiered edifice has a façade of pink granite and local limestone. The famous Bacardí bat tops a pyramidal bell-tower. ◈ *Map V5*
• *Av. Monserrate 261, Habana Vieja*

Palacio Presidencial
4 The lavish eclecticism of the former presidential palace was intended to signify pomp. The extravagant three-story building is topped by a dome and decorated inside with frescoes and mirrors. ◈ *Map W1* • *Calle Refugio 1*

Gran Teatro
5 This theater, built in 1837, is a neo-Baroque confection with corner towers topped by angels, and features sculptures of the muses Charity, Education, Music, and Theater. ◈ *Map W2*
• *Paseo de Martí 452* • *(7) 861 3077*
• *Open 9am–5pm* • *Adm; extra charge for guide*

Hotel Habana Libre
6 Dominating the Vedado skyline, this oblong Modernist tower, built in 1958, features a huge mural in the lobby – *Carro de la Revolución* by Amelia Peláez *(see p40)*. ◈ *Map V1*
• *Calle L & 23*

Edificio Solimar
7 A remarkable example of Art Deco architecture, this huge apartment complex features curvaceous balconies that wrap around the building. ◈ *Map V1*
• *Calle Soledad 205, Centro Habana*

Casa de las Américas
8 Resembling a vertical banded church, this building features a triple-tiered clock-tower. ◈ *Map S1* • *Calle 3ra & Ave. de los Presidentes* • *(7) 838 2707* • *Open 8am–5pm Mon–Fri, 10am–3pm Sat*
• *www.casa.cult.cu*

Tropicana
9 Built around trees and considered the masterpiece of Cuban architect Max Borges Recio, this open-air theater is an exemplar of 1950s *modernismo*.
◈ *Calle 72 & 41, Marianao* • *(7) 267 1717*
• *Open 8:30pm Tue–Sun*
• *www.cabaret-tropicana.com*

Instituto Superior de Artes
10 Designed by three "rebel" architects, this arts school was never completed as it was considered too avant-garde.
◈ *Map T1* • *Calle 120 1110 & 9na, Playa*
• *(7) 208 0017*

Left **Live band at Café París** Right **Peña Obini Batá interior**

Traditional Music Venues

Noches en la Plaza
One Saturday each month, Plaza de la Catedral is closed off and performers put on a colorful show for tourists, who are served dinner beneath the stars. ✪ *Map X1 • Restaurant El Patio • (7) 867 1034 • Held one Sat per month from 9pm (check at Restaurant El Patio for next one)*

Peña Obini Batá
The Asociación Cultural Yoruba de Cuba hosts this *santería*-inspired gathering with traditional music and dance. ✪ *Map W1 • Paseo de Martí 615 • (7) 863 5953 • Held 9pm Fri • Adm*

Sábado de la Rumba
Cuba's premier Afro-Cuban dance troupe puts on a spell-binding performance as the beat draws people to the dance floor. ✪ *Map S2 • Calle 4 103, Vedado • (7) 830 3060 • Open 3pm Sat • Adm*

Rumba del Callejón de Hamel
This Afro-Cuban rumba takes place at a venue where the walls are painted with murals inspired by *santería*. ✪ *Map U2 • Callejón de Hamel, Centro Habana • (7) 878 1661 • Open noon–3pm Sun*

Azotea de Dulce María
This family-run establishment overlooks the Plaza de la Catedral and features traditional Cuban music variants including *son* and *guanguancó*. ✪ *Map W4 • Calle San Ignacio 78, Habana Vieja • (7) 867 1624 • Open 9pm Mon • Adm*

Hurón Azul
Performances of Afro-Cuban music at the Union of Writers and Artists has a lovely setting for performances that draws a bohemian crowd. ✪ *Map T1 • Calle 17 351, Vedado • (7) 832 4551 • Open 5pm–2am daily • Adm*

Casa de la Amistad
Sip *mojitos* and smoke a cigar while enjoying live performances of *danzón, son,* and other music on the patio of this lovely mansion. ✪ *Map S2 • Paseo 406, Vedado • (7) 830 3114 • Open nightly • Adm*

Café París
With a live band, this café-bar is a great place to mingle with Cubans. *Guantanamera* is one of the well-known *son* tunes that you are likely to hear. ✪ *Map X5 • Calle San Ignacio 202, Habana Vieja • (7) 862 0466 • Open 24 hours*

Café Taberna
Occupying a restored 18th-century mansion, this restaurant has a house band and a nine-piece *conjunto* that play here nightly. ✪ *Map X5 • Calle Mercaderes 531, Habana Vieja • (7) 861 1637 • Open 11am–midnight daily*

Wemilere African Roots Festival
This annual festival celebrates Afro-Cuban traditions with lively performances hosted in parks, cultural institutions, and on the streets. ✪ *Held mid–Nov*

Left **Cabaret Parisién** Right **Gato Tuerto neon sign**

🔟 Nightclubs and Cabarets

1 Tropicana
This sensational cabaret billed as "Paradise Under the Stars" is held in an open-air auditorium, where scantily clad showgirls in fanciful, ruffled costumes parade under the treetops *(see p69)*.

2 Cabaret Parisién
Flamboyantly adorned performers release plenty of pent-up energy at this lavish Las Vegas-style cabaret with a distinctly Cuban feel. ❧ *Map U1 • Calle O & 21, Vedado • (7) 836 3663 • Open 9pm nightly • Adm*

3 Jazz Café
Cuba's top jazz performers pack this nightclub that gets in the groove around midnight. Award-winning pianist Chucho Valdés is the resident artiste. ❧ *Map S1 • Calle 1ra & Paseo, Vedado • (7) 838 3556 • Open noon–2am • Adm*

4 Gato Tuerto
Hear everything from *bolero* to *nueva trova* and rap at this intimate supper-club. Locals are known to arrive early for seating. ❧ *Map U1 • Calle O & 19, Vedado • (7) 838 2696 • Open 8pm–3am • Adm*

5 Habana Café
This retro-themed club includes 1950s American automobiles and an airplane suspended from the ceiling. ❧ *Map S1 • Paseo & 3ra, Vedado • (7) 833 3636 ext 147 • Open 8pm–2:30am • Adm for bands*

6 La Zorra y El Cuervo
Named for the fox and the rabbit, top-ranked artists play at what is considered Havana's premier jazz club. ❧ *Map U1 • Calle 23, Vedado • (7) 833 2402 • Open 10pm–2am • Adm • zorra@cbcan.cyt.cu*

7 Salón Turquino
Salsa and other sizzling Latin sounds tempt patrons onto the dance floor of this classy night-club. The resident band is excellent. ❧ *Map U1 • Calle L & 23, Vedado • (7) 838 4011 • Open 10:30pm–3am • Adm • Couples only*

8 Macumba Habana
This venue on the city's outskirts draws a well-heeled crowd. A nightly cabaret is followed by a disco. ❧ *Calle 222 between 37 & 51, La Coronela • (7) 273 0568 • Open 5–11pm Thu, Sat & Sun • Adm*

9 Salón Rosado Benny Moré
Big salsa bands perform on weekends at this vast outdoor concert arena that is popular with Cuban youth. The dancing is no-holds-barred. ❧ *Av. 41 & Calle 48, Reparto Kohly • (7) 206 1282 • Open 7pm–2am Fri–Mon • Adm*

10 La Maison
Fashion shows featuring Cuba's most beautiful models are integrated into a cabaret that is held in the courtyard of Havana's top fashion boutique. ❧ *Calle 16 701, Miramar • (7) 204 1543 • Open 9pm–3am • Adm*

Left **Restaurante Santo Ángel** Center **La Paella** Right **Restaurante El Paseo**

State Restaurants

1 La Bodeguita del Medio
A charming *bodega*-style bar and restaurant serving traditional Cuban dishes, notably roast pork, accompanied by one of La Bodeguita's renowned *mojitos*. ◎ *Map W4 • Calle Empedrado 207, Habana Vieja • (7) 866 8857 • $$*

2 Restaurante Santo Ángel
The Santo Ángel offers excellent nouvelle Cuban cuisine, which can be enjoyed on a patio overlooking Plaza Vieja as musicians entertain. ◎ *Map X5 • Calle Brasil & San Ignacio, Habana Vieja • (7) 861 1626 • $$$*

3 Restaurante El Paseo
Try the monkfish ravioli with sweet pepper sauce at this elegant restaurant. El Paseo has a menu of creative dishes using traditional ingredients. ◎ *Map W4 • Hotel NH Parque Central, Calle Neptuno & Prado • (7) 860 6627 • $$$$*

4 La Paella
A great lunch spot in Habana Vieja, this historic, Spanish-themed restaurant is best known for its *paella* that can be washed down with sangría. ◎ *Map X5 • Calle Oficios 53, Habana Vieja • (7) 867 1037 • $$*

5 Restaurante Biki
Vegetarians are offered unusually creative fare at this buffet-restaurant serving dishes like stuffed eggplant, and fresh juices. ◎ *Map U1 • Calle Infanta & San Lázaro, Centro Habana • (7) 879 6406 • $*

6 Comedor de Aguiar
Resplendent and glittering, this upscale restaurant specializes in international dishes, including a delicious smoked salmon with capers. ◎ *Map U1 • Calle O & 21, Vedado • (7) 836 3564 • $$$$$*

7 La Piazza Ristorante
The best Italian restaurant in town serves almost two dozen types of pizza and above-average pasta dishes. ◎ *Map S1 • Hotel Meliá Cohiba, Paseo & Calle 1ra, Vedado • (7) 833 3636 • $$$*

8 El Aljibe
This busy thatched restaurant serves a signature all-you-can-eat roast chicken with extras. The well-trained staff are always on their toes. ◎ *Av. 7ma & 24, Miramar • (7) 204 1583 • $$*

9 Don Cangrejo
An oceanfront setting is appropriate for Havana's premier seafood restaurant which is popular with government figures. Crab is a house specialty, but lobster, shrimp, and fish dishes fill up the menu. ◎ *Av. 1ra & 16, Miramar • (7) 204 4169*

10 Fusión El Abanico
Deep pockets and nice dresses are required at this sophisticated restaurant in the Hotel Meliá Cohiba. The dishes are nouvelle cuisine. ◎ *Map S1 • Hotel Meliá Cohiba, Paseo & Calle 1ra, Vedado • (7) 833 3636 • $$$$*

Around Cuba – Havana

Price Categories

For a three-course	**$** under CUC$100
meal with half a bottle	**$$** CUC$100–175
of wine or equivalent	**$$$** CUC$175–250
including taxes and	**$$$$** CUC$250–325
extra charges.	**$$$$$** over CUC$325

Left **Paladar Vistamar**

Private Restaurants

1 La Moneda Cubana
This establishment's walls are festooned with personal business cards of patrons. Serves filling portions of simple Cuban chicken, pork, and fish dishes. ◎ *Map X1 • Calle San Ignacio 77, Habana Vieja • (7) 867 3852 • $*

2 Doña Blanquita
Huge portions of basic *criollo* dishes are served on the balcony overlooking Paseo de Martí. ◎ *Map W4 • Paseo de Martí 158, Habana Vieja • (7) 867 4958 • $$*

3 La Guarida
Superb bohemian ambience, excellent French-inspired cuisine, and a one-of-a-kind setting make this the best *paladar* (private restaurant) *(see p125)* in town. ◎ *Map V1 • Calle Concordia 418, Centro Habana • (7) 866 9047 • $$$*
• Reservations essential

4 El Guajirito
The candle-lit countryside atmosphere draws diners to this restaurant on the first floor of an old building near the train station in Old Havana. The *ropa vieja (see p56)* is a must. ◎ *Map W6 • Zulueta 658 (1st floor), Habana Vieja • (7) 862 2760 • $$*

5 Hostal Doña Carmela
Located close to a fortress where cannons are fired nightly, this hostel offers exquisite food, including seafood, among the tropical vegetation of its backyard. ◎ *Map X1 • Com. 1, Casa 10, La Cabaña, Habana del Este • (7) 867 7472 • $$*

6 Gringo Viejo
Adorned with pictures of famous patrons, this atmospheric restaurant serves a superb *ropa vieja* and *flan (see p57)*. Popular with locals and tourists. ◎ *Map T2 • Calle 21 454, Vedado • (7) 831 1946 • $$*

7 La Esperanza
A gracious middle-class mansion with period furnishings and soothing music. French-inspired dishes including chicken and eggplant in honey are served here. ◎ *Calle 16 105, Miramar • (7) 202 4361 • Open Mon–Sat for dinner only • $$$ • Reservations required*

8 Cocina de Lilliam
Lilliam, the owner, whips up creative Cuban dishes such as *ropa vieja* . Choose to eat in either the air-conditioned interior or the charming garden with fairy-lights. ◎ *Calle 48 1311, Miramar • (7) 209 6514 • $$$*

9 Paladar Vistamar
Set above the waves, Paladar Vistamar's wide menu ranges from Cuban staples to international dishes. The grilled fish with garlic is a safe bet. ◎ *Av. 1ra 2206, Miramar • (7) 203 8328 • $$$*

10 Mi Jardín
A Mexican-Italian couple create Mexican fare in their home full of knick-knacks. Patio dining is available beneath an arbor. ◎ *Calle 66 517, Miramar • (7) 203 4627 • $$*

Most private restaurants are open from 12:30pm to 12:30am.

Left **Taller Experimental de la Gráfica** Center **Art at Galería Forma** Right **Tin soldiers**

Shopping

1 Calle Tacón
The Feria de la Artesanía is the city's largest, liveliest, and most colorful artisans' market. Browse for art, sculptures, lacework, and charming papier-mâché figurines. ® Map W4
• Calle Tacón, Habana Vieja

2 Galería Forma
Some of the most creative art, craft, and jewelry is sold here. The bold paintings and copper sculptures are especially appealing. ® Map W5 • Calle Obispo 255, Habana Vieja • (7) 862 0123

3 Taller Experimental de la Gráfica
This is the place to buy unique, limited edition prints hot off the press and you can select from a vast collection of lithographs.
® Map X4 • Callejón del Chorro, Plaza de la Catedral, Habana Vieja

4 Havana 1791
This charming perfume store sells brand-name imported perfumes with twelve local fragrances made on site. ® Map X5 • Calle Mercaderes 156, Habana Vieja • (7) 861 3525

5 El Quitrín
Find hand-embroidered lace blouses and skirts for ladies and traditional guayabera shirts for men. ® Map X5 • Calle Obispo 163, Habana Vieja • (7) 862 0810

6 Tienda El Soldadito de Plomo
An unusual shop where you can buy tiny lead soldiers made on-site as well as miniatures of famous characters such as Charlie Chaplin. ® Map X5
• Calle Muralla 164, Habana Vieja

7 Joyería La Habanera
Antique jewelry and funky contemporary pieces using re-cycled silverware and black coral are available here. ® Calle 12 505, Miramar • (7) 204 2546

8 Calle Obispo
A narrow pedestrian-only street usually abuzz with shoppers browsing art galleries, bookstores, and boutiques. Beware of pickpockets. ® Map W5–X4 • Calle Obispo, Habana Vieja

9 Casa de la Música EGREM
EGREM, the state recording company, has the largest selection of music CDs, DVDs, and cassettes in town. Prices, however, are no bargain.
® Calle 20 3309, Miramar • (7) 204 0447
• www.egrem.com.cu

10 Casa Verano
Shop here for quality imported and Cuban-designed clothes and accessories, that include trademark Verano dresses and straw hats. ® Calle 18 4706, Playa • (7) 204 1982

Left **Museo del Tabaco** Right **Neon sign at the Fábrica de Tabacos Partagás cigar factory**

🔟 Cigar Venues

1 Fábrica de Tabacos Partagás
See fine cigars being rolled and check out a well-stocked humidor with a VIP room. ◎ *Map W2 • Calle Industria 520, Centro Habana • (7) 862 0086 • Open 9am–2:30pm Mon–Fri*

2 Museo del Tabaco
Displaying paraphernalia relating to smoking, this small museum has a small cigar shop downstairs. ◎ *Map X5 • Calle Mercaderes 120, Habana Vieja • (7) 861 5795 • Open 9am–5pm Tue–Sat*

3 Hostal Conde de Villanueva
The sumptuous lounge and waiter service makes this a great place to sample cigars. ◎ *Map X5 • Calle Mercaderes 202, Habana Vieja • (7) 862 9294 • Open 10am–7pm*

4 Café Barrita
A hidden gem, this small Art Deco bar offers strong cocktails. It sells a small selection of smokes by day only and is a popular place for cigar-lovers. ◎ *Map V5 • Edificio Bacardí, Calle Monserrate 261, Habana Vieja • (7) 862 9310 • Open 9am–6pm Mon–Sat*

5 Fábrica de Tabacos Romeo y Julieta
This famous cigar factory has been in operation since 1875. It offers tours of the factory and stocks a wide range of cigars. ◎ *Map • Calle Belascoaín 852, Centro Habana • (7) 878 1058 • Open 8:30–11am & noon–3pm Mon–Fri*

6 Salón Cuaba
Salón Cuaba caters to serious smokers with an elegant smoking lounge and waiter bar service. The staff is knowledgeable. ◎ *Map V5 • Hotel Parque Central, Calle Neptuno & Zulueta • (7) 860 6627 • Open 8:30am–9:15pm*

7 Festival del Habano
Attracting celebrities and cigar-lovers, this festival features concerts and a grand finale auction with humidors signed by Fidel Castro. ◎ *(7) 204 0510 • February • www.habanos.com*

8 Club Habana
This private members' club is run by cigar maestro Enrique Mons, Cuba's most knowledgeable cigar expert. ◎ *5ta Av. between 188 and 192, Playa • (7) 204 5700 • Open 9am–11pm*

9 Casa del Habano
An upscale store with a huge humidor stocked with the finest Cohibas, Romeo y Julietas, and other top brands. Smoke comfortably in the lounge and bar. ◎ *5ta Av. & Calle 16, Miramar • (7) 204 7975 • Open 10am–6pm Mon–Sat*

10 Fábrica de Tabacos El Laguito
Aficionados who prefer robust Cohibas, Cuba's flagship brand, may want to buy them at the factory where they're made. The Trinidad label is also hand-rolled here. ◎ *Av. 146 2302, Cubanacán • (7) 208 2218 • By appointment*

Left **Cayo Levisa** Right **Façade of the Presidio Modelo**

Western Cuba

WESTERN CUBA BOASTS SOME OF THE MOST BEAUTIFUL *scenery in the country. The dramatic beauty reaches its pinnacle at Pinar del Río in the Viñales valley. These mountains are laced with hiking trails, notably at mountain communities Soroa and Las Terrazas, and in the Guanahacabibes Peninsula, at the western tip of Cuba. Fine tobacco is grown in fields tucked into valleys and spread throughout the Vuelta Abajo region. Just off the mainland is Isla de la Juventud, with an expanse of wild terrain that shelters endemic bird life. Neighboring Cayo Largo, an island in the Archipiélago de los Canarreos, with its white beaches, is a tourist-only haven.*

Boats moored at Cayo Largo

🔟 Sights

1. Las Terrazas
2. Soroa
3. Viñales
4. Cayo Levisa
5. Pinar del Rio
6. Vuelta Abajo
7. Parque Nacional Península de Guanahacabibes
8. Cayo Largo
9. Nueva Gerona
10. Presidio Modelo

Preceding pages **Vista over Valle de Viñales**

Farmer ploughing a field with oxen near Viñales

Viñales

The agricultural community of Viñales has preserved the colonial architecture of this tiny village. The main street is lined with red-tile, roofed cottages fronted by columned arcades. The nearby Casa de Don Tomás, an architectural gem built in 1822, has been converted into a restaurant. A church stands over Parque Martí, where the Casa de la Cultura hosts cultural activities. It is common to see horse-drawn carts making their way through town toward the tobacco fields and *mogotes* nearby *(see p13)*. ◈ Map B2 • Casa de Don Tomás: Calle Salvador Cisneros 140; (48) 79 6300 • Casa de la Cultura: Calle José Martí 5; (48) 77 8128; adm

Las Terrazas

Founded in 1968 as a village in the pine-clad mountains of the eastern Sierra del Rosario, this community *(see p12)* has a lovely setting with simple houses built in terraces overlooking a lake. The local Hotel La Moka focuses on ecotourism and arranges bird and hiking trips. The village also hosts local rodeo entertainment. Tourists can walk the well-maintained trails that lead to the Buena Vista coffee plantation and along the San Juan river to cascades and mineral springs. Boats can also be hired on the lake. ◈ Map C2 • Hotel La Moka: Autopista Nacional, km 51, Pinar del Río; (48) 57 8600 • www.lasterrazas.cu

Soroa

Surrounded by forested mountains, Soroa, once a center for coffee production, is currently a holiday village offering a scenic escape for nature lovers. Attractions include a stunning orchid garden *(see p12)* displaying more than 700 species. A trail heads sharply downhill to the El Salto waterfall, while more challenging hikes lead to the Mirador de Venus – a mountain-top lookout with superlative views. The Hotel & Villa Turística Soroa is a simple, though delightful, retreat. ◈ Map C2 • Hotel & Villa Turística Soroa: (48) 52 3534

Cayo Levisa

Ringed by white-sand beaches, this tiny island *(see p48)* off Pinar del Río can be reached by a small ferry from the mainland. A nearby coral reef has splendid crystal-clear dive sites while the deeper waters farther offshore are populated with marlin and other game-fish. The mangroves found in this region are also a habitat for waterbirds *(see p48)*.

Flowers in the orchid garden in Soroa

The Palacio de Guasch at Pinar del Río

5 Pinar del Río

Founded in 1669, this is a peaceful town with a sloping main street lined with eclectic buildings, many with Art Nouveau façades. The Palacio de Guasch stands out for its flamboyant exterior. The town is a center of tobacco processing and is home to the Fábrica de Tabacos Francisco Donatién, the local cigar factory. ⊗ *Map B3 • Fábrica de Tabacos Francisco Donatién: (48) 773 069; open 9am–4pm Mon–Fri, 9am–noon Sat; adm*

6 Vuelta Abajo

To the west of the provincial capital, these fertile plains centered on the town of San Juan y Martínez are famed for their tobacco. The leaves, protected from the sun by fine netting, are cured in traditional ranches. The Finca El Pinar Vegas Robaina, a private tobacco *finca* (ranch) of renowned farmer Alejandro Robaina is worth a visit. ⊗ *Map B3 • Finca El Pinar San Luis, Vegas Robaina • (48) 79 7470 • Open 10am–5pm Mon–Sat • Adm for guided tours*

Cork Palm

Found only in a few tiny pockets of the Sierra del Rosario, Cuba's endemic *Palma corcho* is a primitive member of the cycad family. Living in an ecosystem threatened by deforestation, the species reproduces with difficulty, although individual palms live to be more than 300 years. As a result, this living fossil faces possible extinction.

7 Parque Nacional Península de Guanahacabibes

Occupying a slender peninsula jutting into the Gulf of Mexico at the western tip of Cuba, this park *(see p46)* – a UNESCO Biosphere Reserve – protects a rare dry forest habitat. Endangered mammals like the endemic hutia and solenodon exist here, as do deer, wild pigs, iguanas, and more than 170 bird species. Guided hikes are offered from the Ecological Station. A sandy track runs to Cabo San Antonio, marked by a lighthouse built in 1849. ⊗ *Map A3 • (48) 75 0366 • Adm • www.ecovida-pinar.cu*

8 Cayo Largo

Lined with a series of white-sand beaches, Cayo Largo offers activites like horseback riding, sailing and scuba diving. Excursions whisk you off to nearby isles that are home to flamingos and iguanas. Accommodations range from a fishing lodge to 4-star all-inclusives *(see p124)*. The island is popular for excursions from Havana and Varadero. ⊗ *Map F4*

Hanging tobacco to dry at Vuelta Abajo

For contact information about excursions to Cayo Largo See p126

Nueva Gerona

The slightly sleepy capital city of Isla de la Juventud has a graceful colonial core featuring venerable one-story buildings with columns supporting red-tiled roofs. The Iglesia Nuestra Señora de los Dolores is a lovely church on the remodeled main plaza, which has a small museum. The Museo de Ciencias Naturales nearby displays re-creations of local natural habitats. ⊗ *Map D4*
• *Iglesia Nuestra Señora de los Dolores: (46) 32 3791; hours vary* • *Museo de Ciencias Naturales: (46) 32 3143; open Tue–Sat 9:30am–noon, 1–5pm, Sun 8am–noon; adm*

Presidio Modelo at Nueva Gerona

Presidio Modelo

This former penitentiary *(see p32)* on the southeast outskirts of Nueva Gerona was built in 1926 with three huge circular cellblocks. In October 1953, Fidel Castro and 25 other revolutionaries were imprisoned here following their failed attack on the Moncada barracks *(see pp30 – 31)*. These days, the prison hospital functions as a museum recalling the 20 months that Castro and the other revolutionaries spent here. Castro's room features a collection of books he read, using them to instruct fellow prisoners.
⊗ *Map D4* • *(46) 32 5112* • *Open 8am–4pm Tue–Sat; 8am–noon Sun* • *Adm (extra charge for cameras)*

North Coast Drive

Morning

Leave Havana in a rental car and head west along Avenue 5ta, which leads past the Latin American School for Medical Sciences, where international students receive free medical training. Pass through the port town of Mariel, onto Carretera 2-1-3, a winding and gently rolling road frequented by ox-drawn carts. After about two hours of driving past sugarcane fields, turn south at the sign for **Soroa** *(see p79)* and follow the road as it curls uphill through pine forest. Take the time to explore the orchid garden and hike the short trail to the Cascadas El Salto waterfall. Enjoy lunch at one of the restaurants in the locale before continuing.

Afternoon

Returning to the highway, continue west through the towns of Bahía Honda and Las Pozas, with the Sierra del Rosario mountains to the south. The Pan de Guajaibón – a dramatic *mogote* can be reached by turning south at the hamlet of Rancho Canelo. Further west beyond Las Pozas, turn north for the ferry dock to **Cayo Levisa** *(see p79)* where you can enjoy an overnight stay at a charming hotel. Boats depart at 10am and 6pm. Alternatively, continue west beyond La Palma to **Viñales** *(see p13)*. The road cuts through tobacco fields before emerging in the Valle de San Vicente. Turn south at the T-junction for **Viñales**. Two affordable hotels sit atop *mogotes*; and private rooms *(casas particulares)* are available.

Left **Cueva de los Portales** Right **Criadero de Cocodrilos**

Best of the Rest

1 San Antonio de los Baños
This small colonial town has a humor museum and echoes with laughter during the Bienal del Humor comedy festival every two years. ✎ Map C2

2 Cueva de los Portales
A dramatic cavern full of dripstone formations, which Che Guevara made his headquarters during the Cuban Missile Crisis *(see p12).*

3 María la Gorda
This remote and popular dive spot at the far west end of Cuba is set on a gorgeous bay full of coral and other marine life. ✎ Map A4

4 Cuevas de Puntas del Este
A permit is required to visit these caves adorned with ancient Taíno pictographs. ✎ Map D4 • c/o Ecotur: Calle 24 and 31, Nueva Gerona; (46) 32 7101

5 Gran Caverna de Santo Tomás
In the heart of a *mogote*-studded valley, the Saint Thomas caves form the largest underground system in Cuba *(see p13).* ✎ Map B2 • 20 miles (32 km) west of Viñales • Guided tours are offered

6 Playa Jibacoa
Jibacoa is a series of beaches that are popular with Cuban families. The government is planning to develop the zone for tourists as well. ✎ Map E2

7 Criadero de Cocodrilos
Cuba's endemic crocodile is raised here for reintroduction into the wild. Visit in the early morning to witness feeding time. ✎ Map D4 • c/o Ecotur: Calle 24 and 31, Nueva Gerona; (46) 32 7101; a guide is compulsory

8 Reserva Ecológica Los Indios
These mangroves, grasslands, and forests on the southwest shores of Isla de la Juventud teem with wildlife. ✎ Map C4 • c/o Ecotur: Calle 24 and 31, Nueva Gerona; (46) 32 7101; a guide is compulsory

9 Museo Finca El Abra
This simple colonial-era farm was where José Martí stayed during his house arrest in 1870. It is now a museum. ✎ Map D4 • Carretera Siguanea, km 2 • Open 9am–4pm Tue–Sat, 9am–1pm Sun • Adm

10 Parque Nacional Punta Francés
At the southwest tip of Isla de la Juventud, the stunning coral formations and numerous wrecks make this national park a superb spot for diving. ✎ Map C4

Left **Cueva del Indio in Valle de Viñales** Center **Fishing off Havana harbor** Right **Horseback riding**

Outdoor Activities

Hiking
Las Terrazas and Soroa *(see p12)* are perfect places for walking, whether it's short strolls or challenging hikes. The two hotels located here can arrange guides for visitors who are more ambitious *(see p132)*.

Horseback Riding
The region may not be well equipped for horseback riding, but it is possible to rent horses behind the beach at Playa Blanca on Cayo Largo *(see p81)*. ⚲ *Reservations can be made at Hotel Isla del Sur • Adm*

Caving
This cave is the place to go for those who want to explore Cuba's hidden depths. The Centro Nacional de Espeleología can arrange visits for serious cavers. ⚲ *Centro Nacional de Espeleología • Booking can be made at Hotel Los Jazmines: Carretera a Viñales, km 23; (48) 79 6205*

Diving
Acclaimed for the finest diving in Cuba, La Costa de los Piratas (the Pirate Coast) off Punta Francés *(see p82)* offers dozens of fantastic dive sites – including the opportunity to explore the wrecks of several sunken Spanish galleons.

Cycling
The dramatic scenery and peaceful, paved roads of the Valle de Viñales *(see p46)* guarantee cyclists an experience to remember. Local farmers offer a warm welcome.

Bird-Watching
The Guanahacabibes Peninsula is home to more than 170 bird species, including a number of endemics best seen on guided hikes through the preserve. ⚲ *Estación Ecológica, Parque Nacional Guanahacabibes • (48) 75 0366 • osmanibf@yahoo.es*

Rock-Climbing
Scaling the *mogotes* of the Valle de Viñales requires skill; more than 100 established climbs have been pioneered by local enthusiasts.

Swimming
The waters surrounding Cayo Levisa are ideal for swimming and snorkeling, and the lakes at Las Terrazas *(see p12)* are great for refreshing dips. ⚲ *Cayo Levisa • (48) 75 6501*

Wildlife Viewing
View various types of fauna and bird-life including flamingos, iguanas, and monkeys that inhabit the remote cays west of Cayo Largo, from where excursions are offered.

Fishing
The waters off Cayo Largo offer anglers plenty of thrills from tiny but challenging bonefish to marlin, which put up a rod-bending fight.

Left **Mangroves** Right **Turtles**

📑10 Wildlife

Mangroves
Growing at the boundary of land and sea, mangroves form a tangled web of interlocking roots that rise from the waters and provide shelter for juvenile marine creatures. Five species grow in Cuba along both Caribbean and Atlantic shores.

Crocodiles
The swamplands of southern Isla de la Juventud harbor a large population of Cuban crocodiles *(see p50)*. A successful breeding program has brought the species back from the edge of extinction.

Turtles
Female marine turtles crawl onto the shores of pristine Cuban beaches to lay their eggs above the high-water mark. A farm on Isla de la Juventud specializes in breeding green and hawksbill turtles.

Parrots
Cuba's endemic parrot *(see p50)* is easily recognized with its red cheeks, white forehead, and blue wing-tips. The dry tropical forests of Isla de la Juventud have the largest parrot population in Cuba.

Spoonbills
This rose-colored wading bird has a spatulate bill and is a member of the Ibis family. It nests in mangroves and can be seen in the Refugio Ecológico Los Indios *(see p82)*.

Whale Sharks
Scuba divers often have close encounters with whale sharks in the warm waters of the Bahía de Corrientes and off Punta Francés.

Bonefish
This silvery fish is well-camouflaged against the sandy bottoms of shallow lagoons and is notorious for the challenging fight it gives anglers. Cayo Largo is a prime site for bonefishing.

Marlin
The fast-flowing Gulf Stream off the north coast of Pinar del Río is a veritable highway for marlin, which give sport-fishers a tremendous fight. María La Gorda has a marina and offers sport-fishing charters. ✆ *María La Gorda: (82) 77 1306*

Iguanas
Looking almost as lifeless as the ground they walk on, these giant lizards *(see p50)* crawl around the arid terrain of the Península de Guanahacabibes *(see p46)* and the infertile Archipiélago de los Canarreos.

Manatees
These endangered marine mammals inhabit the coastal lagoons off both north and south shores and, although rarely seen, are very common off the Golfo de Guanahacabibes. Manatees feed on seabed grasses and other vegetation.

Coppelia ice-cream parlor sign

Price Categories

For a three-course		$ under CUC\$100
meal with half a bottle		\$\$ CUC\$100–175
of wine or equivalent		\$\$\$ CUC\$175–250
including taxes and		\$\$\$\$ CUC\$250–325
extra charges.		\$\$\$\$\$ over CUC\$325

🔟 Restaurants

La Fondita de Mercedes
This *paladar* (private restaurant) serves traditional Cuban meals in a family environment. The marinated braised lamb is delicious; wash it down with local Soroa wine. You can dine on a terrace overlooking a lake. ◈ *Map C2 • Casa 9, Las Terrazas • c/o (48) 57 8600 • \$\$*

Casa del Campesino
A real farmstead where traditional Cuban dishes are prepared in an outdoor oven and enjoyed under a thatched roof. Popular with tour groups. ◈ *Map C2 • Las Terrazas • c/o (48) 57 8555 • \$\$*

Restaurante Rumayor
Although the *criollo* dishes served here are average, this thatched restaurant is fascinating for its Tiki-style decor and African drums. Stay for the evening cabaret. ◈ *Map B3 • Av. a Viñales, Pinar del Río town • (48) 76 3007 • \$\$*

Coppelia
A perfect place to beat the heat, this ice-cream parlor gets packed with local families who want to indulge. ◈ *Map B3 • Calle Medina Norte 33, Pinar del Río • \$*

Restaurante Las Arcadas
This hotel restaurant has a lovely, airy ambience, and overlooks lush grounds. It serves seafood, spaghetti, and Cuban staples. ◈ *Map B2 • Rancho San Vicente, Carretera a Puerto Esperanza, km 33 • (48) 79 6201 • \$\$*

Casa de Don Tomás
A historic building where musicians play traditional tunes. The house special is *delicias de Don Tomás*, a pork, chicken, and lobster dish, served with rice, beans, and *tostones* (fried plantains). ◈ *Map B2 • Calle Salvador Cisneros 147, Viñales • (48) 79 6300 • \$\$*

Hotel Los Jazmines
Overlooking the Valle de Viñales from atop a *mogote (see p102)*, this location offers the most dramatic view of any restaurant in Cuba. ◈ *Map B2 • Carretera de Viñales, km 25 • (48) 79 6205 • \$\$*

Casa del Veguero
Set amid tobacco fields, this thatched open-air restaurant serves prix fixe *criollo* meals and includes tours of the tobacco farm. Musicians entertain while you eat. ◈ *Map B2 • Viñales • (48) 79 6080 • \$\$\$*

Restaurante La Moka
This is an elegant place to enjoy lobster dishes and specialties such as delicious roast chicken. ◈ *Map C2 • Hotel La Moka, Las Terrazas • (48) 57 8600 • \$\$\$*

Restaurante Centro
A reasonable buffet is served at this hotel restaurant along with à la carte dishes that include seafood, pasta, and *criollo* fare, such as *ropa vieja (see p56)*. Musicians provide entertainment. ◈ *Map C2 • Hotel & Villa Turística Soroa • (48) 52 3534 • \$\$*

Left **Mansión Xanadú**, Varadero Right **Colonades in the main square at Remedios**

Central Cuba West

Encompassing the provinces of Matanzas, Cienfuegos, and Santa Clara, Central Cuba West is the traditional center of tourism. Visitors flock to the white sands of Varadero, and even further east, Cayo Santa María is fast developing into a booming tourist beach spot. The region is also blessed with wilderness – the Zapata Peninsula shelters crocodiles and birdlife, while the pine-clad Sierra del Escambray offers mountain trails and waterfalls. History fans are drawn to museums at Playa Girón and Santa Clara. Cienfuegos is blessed with imposing colonial structures and fin de siècle mansions, while Matanzas thrums to the rhythms of Afro-Cuban music and dance. At Christmas, the sleepy town of Remedios explodes with fireworks fever.

🔟 Sights

1. Matanzas
2. Varadero
3. Cárdenas
4. Parque Nacional Ciénaga de Zapata
5. Santa Clara
6. Remedios
7. Cayo Santa María
8. Cienfuegos
9. Sierra del Escambray
10. Caibarién

Cayo Santa María

Matanzas

1 This historic port town, which evolved as a center for sugar export and importation of slaves, was dubbed the "Athens of Cuba," when artistic life flourished here during the 19th century. Most sites of interest surround Plaza de la Vigía, including the Teatro Sauto and the Catedral de San Carlos. Visit San Severino castle's slave-trade museum and, outside town, Cuevas de Bellamar's caverns. 🚫 *Map E2 • Teatro Sauto: Plaza de la Vigía; (45) 24 2721; open Tue–Sun daily; adm • Castillo de San Severino: Zona Industrial; (45) 28 3259; open 8:30am–4:30pm Tue–Sat, 8:30am–12:30pm Sun; adm*

Teatro Sauto, Matanzas

Varadero

2 Cuba's top resort, its beach offers plenty of watersports, but shade is in short supply. Most hotels here are all-inclusive, but visitors can also choose from a handful of smaller options. Golfers can tee off at an 18-hole course at Mansión Xanadú *(see p133)*. Regional attractions include hiking, scuba diving, and a dolphin show. 🚫 *Map F2 • Dolphin shows: Carretera Las Morlas, km 11.5; (45) 66 8031*

Cárdenas

3 The somewhat run-down port town of Cárdenas offers a fistful of intriguing attractions. A good starting point is tiny Parque Colón, where a statue of Christopher Columbus stands in front of the browbeaten Catedral de la Concepción Inmaculada, built in 1826. The Museo Municipal Oscar María de Rojas *(see p37)* has fascinating displays with some artifacts dating back to pre-Columbian days. Horse-drawn taxi-cabs traverse town, and are a great way to sightsee and meet locals. 🚫 *Map F2*

Parque Nacional Ciénaga de Zapata

4 This vast park is Cuba's most complete wildlife preserve. Swampland smothers the region, while mangroves, reeds, and wet forests also provide varied habitats that support more than 200 bird species, including the Cuban pygmy owl and the tiny endemic *zunzuncito (see p50)*. Manatees swim in coastal lagoons, where Cuban crocodiles also lurk, and flamingos flock to Laguna de las Salinas at the head of the Bahía de Cochinos *(see p14)*. Official guides lead nature-oriented tours. The few inhabitants have traditionally made a living by burning mangroves to make charcoal. 🚫 *Map E3 • National Park office: Playa Larga; (45) 98 7249; open 8am–4:30pm daily; adm includes a guide*

Mangrove swamp, Parque Nacional Ciénaga de Zapata

Manjuarí
This primitive fish from the ante-diluvian dawn evolved at least 270 million years ago, about the time the first reptiles crawled out of the seas. Growing to 6 ft (2 m) long, it has an elongated snout like a crocodile's. Its scaly skin is covered with natural oil. Endemic to Cuba, the dark green fish inhabits the Zapata swamps.

Santa Clara
5 Known as the "city of the heroic guerrilla," Santa Clara is an industrial and university town from where, in 1958, Che Guevara led the final battle to topple Batista *(see p32)*. Visitors flock to sites associated with the battle, such as the Tren Blindado (a derailed armoured train) and the Complejo Escultórico Ernesto Che Guevara *(see p91)*. Also of interest is the frescoed ceiling of the Teatro de la Caridad (Charity Theater). ✆ *Map H3 • Teatro de la Caridad, Parque Vidal 3: (45) 20 5548*

Remedios
6 Founded in 1578, this is one of Cuba's most charming colonial cities. Its streets are lined with simple homes featuring nail-studded wooden doors and *rejas*

– barred windows. The Museo de la Música Alejandro García Caturla displays musical instruments and the Museo de las Parrandas gives a foretaste of what's in store during Christmas *(see p53)*. ✆ *Map H3 • Museo de la Música Alejandro García Caturla: (42) 39 6851; open 9am–noon & 1–5pm Tue–Sat, 9am–noon Sun; adm • Museo de las Parrandas: open 9am–noon Tue–Sat, 9am–1pm Sun; adm*

Cayo Santa María
7 This island lies 45 miles (28 km) from the mainland, to which it is connected by a very narrow *pedraplén* (causeway). The calm peacock-blue sea is protected by a coral reef and is ideal for swimming and snorkeling – the deeper waters beyond the reef offer diving. Catamaran and sport-fishing excursions depart from a marina. ✆ *Map J1*

Palacio del Valle, Cienfuegos

Cienfuegos
8 A maritime city lying on the shores of a massive bay, Cienfuegos was founded in 1819, when French settlers laid out a near-perfect grid around the Plaza de Armas, now called Parque Martí. Neo-Classical buildings that grace the square include a restored cathedral. The

A group of sculptures dedicated to Che Guevara, Santa Clara

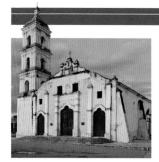

Cathedral at Remedios

tree-shaded Paseo del Prado boulevard slopes to the Punta Gorda district, where accommodation in Art Nouveau and mid-20th-century Modernist homes can be rented. The highlight of any visit is a meal at Palacio del Valle, a mansion decorated in Moorish fashion *(see p93)*.

9 Sierra del Escambray

Spanning three provinces, this rugged mountain range rises inland from the Caribbean coast, attaining 3,790 ft (1,156 m) atop Pico San Juan. Coffee is farmed on the lower slopes, while the densely forested upper slopes are of great ecological value for their plants and profuse birdlife. Topes de Collantes *(see p46)* offers accommodation and is a base for guided nature hikes. Embalse Habanilla, a manmade lake, shimmers on the northern slopes. ⊗ *Map H3*

10 Caibarién

A once-important port town that still lives partly off its humble fishing fleet, sprawling Caibarién has a dishevelled countenance and awaits a renaissance of its incredible wealth of architecture, with buildings from Neo-Classical to Art Nouveau centered on Parque de la Libertad. The town also has beaches, and mangroves teeming with birds. ⊗ *Map H3*

Jagüey Grande to Cienfuegos Drive

Morning

Start your day early with a visit to the **Museo Memorial Comandancia FAR** *(see p14)*. After a brief tour, get to the highway and drive south along the ruler-straight road with the grassy swamps of **Zapata** *(see pp14–15)* on each side. Break at **La Boca de Guamá** to see the crocodiles and then at **Centro Ecológico**, where an ecological trail lets you experience the Zapata ecosystems first-hand. Back at Playa Larga, follow the main road south along the shoreline toward Playa Girón. Take time to browse the fascinating Museo Girón *(see p15)* then continue 5 miles (8 km) east to **Caleta Buena** *(see p15)*. Enjoy lunch and an hour or two snorkeling in this sheltered cove. Note that in March and April, the road is smothered with crabs migrating inland to spawn. They are a hazard; ensure that your tires have plenty of tread to reduce the chance of getting a puncture from broken shells.

Afternoon

Retrace your path to Playa Girón and turn north; the route is potholed in places. At Bermejas, turn right. Observe daily rural Cuban life in the remote settlements you pass through. Turn right onto Carretera 3-1-2, the main highway that leads to the well-planned maritime city of **Cienfuegos**. Spend the rest of the day admiring its Neo-Classical structures, ending with a seafood meal at the exotic **Palacio del Valle** *(see p93)*.

Left **Delfinario** Center **Castillo de Jagua** Right **Fiesta Finca Campesina**

🔟 Best of the Rest

1 Cuevas de Bellamar
These extensive caves have fascinating dripstone features. A small museum located here details the geological processes. ◈ Map E2 • Carretera de las Cuevas de Bellamar • (45) 25 3538 • Open 9:30am–5pm Tue–Sun • Adm • Seven tours daily

2 Museo Playa Girón
This museum, replete with gory photographs and bloody uniforms, recalls the Bay of Pigs invasion (see p31). Displays include a Sea Fury plane (see p15).

3 Fiesta Finca Campesina
This re-creation of a typical Cuban farm has a zoo with crocodiles, a sugarcane press, and buffalo rides. ◈ Map F3 • Autopista Nacional, km 142, Jagüey Grande • (45) 91 2045 • Open 9am–5pm • Adm

4 Delfinario
Bottlenose dolphins and sealions perform acrobatics at this marine park outside Cienfuegos. ◈ Map G3 • Rancho Luna • (43) 54 8120 • Open 8:30am–4pm Thu–Tue • Adm; extra to swim with dolphins

5 Jardín Botánico Soledad
A botanical garden houses one of the world's largest palm collections as well as other exotic plants. ◈ Map G3 • Pepito Tey • (43) 54 5115 • Open 8am–4:30pm • Adm

6 Castillo de Jagua
This tiny fortress guarding the entrance to Cienfuegos Bay still has a working drawbridge across the moat and is believed to be haunted by a lady dressed in blue. ◈ Map G3 • Poblado Castillo de Jagua • (43) 96 5402 • Open 9am–5pm Mon–Sat, 9am–1pm Sun • Adm

7 Lago Hanabanilla
This reservoir on the Sierra del Escambray's northern slopes resembles a jigsaw puzzle. The no-frills Hotel Hanabanilla stands over the western shore. ◈ Map H3 • Hotel Hanabanilla: (42) 25 8550

8 Playa Rancho Luna
Along Cuba's south coast, this attractive beach has two tourist hotels and the Faro Luna dive center. ◈ Map G3 • Faro Luna Dive Center • (43) 54 8040

9 Museo del Vapor
Train buffs will enjoy this collection of antique steam trains, most in a decrepit condition, at Central Maltiempo – a sugar factory and now the setting for an annual steam train festival. ◈ Map G3

10 Boca de Guamá
Beside Laguna del Tesoro, this tourist facility has a crocodile farm and offers boat tours of the lagoon. ◈ Map F3 • (45) 91 5662

Left **El Morrillo** Center **Museo de la Batalla de Ideas** Right **Museo Memorial Comandancia FAR**

TOP 10 Revolutionary Sites

1 Castillo El Morrillo
This fortress houses the mausoleum of revolutionary leaders Antonio Guiteras Holmes and Carlos Aponte Hernández. ◈ *Map F2 • Canímar • Open 9am–4pm Tue–Sun*

2 Museo de la Batalla de Ideas
A museum recalling the custody battle over Elián González, a Cuban boy plucked from sea by Cuban-Americans who refused to return him to Cuba. ◈ *Map F2 Av. 6 between 11 & 12, Cárdenas • Open 9am–5pm Tue–Sun • Adm*

3 Museo Casa Natal de José Antonio Echeverría
This museum was once the home of Echeverría *(see p35)*. ◈ *Map F2 • Genes between Calzada & Coronel Verdugo, Cárdenas • (45) 52 4145 • Open 9am–6pm Tue–Sat • Adm*

4 Museo Playa Girón
The Cuban version of the Bay of Pigs invasion is recounted at this museum *(see p15)*.

5 Playa Larga
On April 17, 1961, CIA-sponsored Cuban exiles landed on this beach. Roadside markers are dedicated to those who died defending it *(see p31)*. ◈ *Map F3*

6 Museo Memorial Comandancia FAR
This museum commemorates Castro's headquarters, which was situated here during the Bay of Pigs invasion *(see p14)*.

7 Complejo Escultórico Ernesto Che Guevara
A statue of Che looms over sculptures at this site, which features the mausoleum where his body is interred *(see p32)*. ◈ *Map H3 • Plaza de la Revolución, Santa Clara • (42) 20 5878 • Open 9:30am–5:30pm Tue–Sat, 9:30am–5pm Sun*

8 Museo Naval
The headquarters of an anti-Batista revolt on September 5, 1957, this is now a naval museum. ◈ *Map G3 • Calle 21 & Av. 62, Cienfuegos • (43) 51 9143 • Open 10am–6pm Tue–Sat, 9am–1pm Sun • Adm*

9 Tren Blindado
This monument re-creates the derailing of an armored train by Che's guerrillas using the original carriages. ◈ *Map H3 • Av. Independencia btwn Línea & Puente de la Cruz, Santa Clara • (42) 20 2758 • Open 9am–5pm Mon–Sat • Adm*

10 Museo Provincial Abel Santamaría
A museum dedicated to the revolutionary movement in Santa Clara is housed in this former military barracks. ◈ *Map H3 • Calle Esquerra • (42) 20 3041 • Open 8am–4:30pm Mon–Fri, 8am–1pm Sat • Adm*

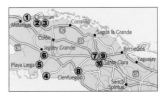

Left **Sailing at Varadero** Center **Horse-Carriage Tour** Right **Varadero's golf course**

Things to Do

1 Sailing

Small sailing boats can be rented at Rancho Luna and Varadero *(see p87)* from where boat trips to outlying cays depart and rum cocktails are served as the sun sets.

2 Scuba Diving

Diving enthusiasts will enjoy the region's north and south shores. Playa Larga *(see p91)*, is famed for its coral reefs, and Varadero for sunken warships.

3 Learning to Dance

Matanzas *(see p87)* is an excellent venue for learning to dance like a Cuban. Festivals in October and November feature dance workshops.

4 Riding the Hershey Train

Connecting Matanzas to Casablanca, this commuter train passes through sugarcane fields once owned by the Hershey chocolate factory.

5 Angling for Bonefish

The region offers some of the best bonefishing in the Caribbean. The shallow lagoons off southern Zapata *(see p87)* and Cayo Santa María *(see p88)* are the best spots. Hotels offer guided fishing trips.

6 Birding

Parque Nacional Ciénaga de Zapata and the Sierra del Escambray teem with exotic bird species. Look for parrots, the tocororo, and zunzuncito *(see p50)*, as well as flamingos in the lagoons of Zapata.

7 Snorkeling at Caleta Buena

The whole region is very good for snorkeling, but this cove *(see p15)* near Playa Girón offers a display of corals, sponges, and tropical fishes. Snorkeling gear can be rented. Lunch and snacks are served during the course of the day. ◈ *Map F3*

8 Horse-Carriage Tour

Formal excursions by colonial-era, horse-drawn carriages are a great way to explore Varadero and Cienfuegos *(see p88)*, while in all other cities you can hop aboard rickety *coches* that ply the main streets as slow-moving taxis for locals.

9 Paragliding

Varadero is the place for this thrilling activity, where you strap on a harness attached to a giant kite pulled by a speedboat. In seconds you're soaring, with a bird's view of the beach resort far below.

10 Golf

The Varadero Golf Club is Cuba's only 18-hole golf course, although more are planned. Laid out along the shore, it offers a breeze-swept challenge between the sands and a lagoon. ◈ *Map F2*
• *Av. Las Américas, km 8.5* • *(45) 66 7788*
• *www.varaderogolfclub.com*

Price Categories

For a three-course meal with half a bottle of wine or equivalent including taxes and extra charges.	**$** under CUC$100
	$$ CUC$100–175
	$$$ CUC$175–250
	$$$$ CUC$250–325
	$$$$$ over CUC$325

Left **Exterior of the El Bodegón Criollo**

🔟 Restaurants

1 Restaurante Guamairé
Try spicy crocodile with pineapple, served with rice and beans at this restaurant housed in an old wooden home. ◈ *Map F2 • Av. 1ra & Calle 27, Varadero • (45) 61 1893 • $$*

2 El Bodegón Criollo
Copying the theme of the famous Bodeguita del Medio in Havana, this modest restaurant offers indoor and outdoor dining. A highlight of the *criollo* dishes is the roast leg of pork. ◈ *Map F2 • Av. de la Playa & Calle 40, Varadero • (45) 66 7784 • $*

3 El Mesón del Quijote
Set atop a grassy hillock, this restaurant re-creates the mood of a Spanish *bodega* with its rustic decor. The menu offers steaks and seafood, including several lobster dishes. ◈ *Map F2 • Av. Las Américas, Varadero • (45) 66 7796 • $$$*

4 Restaurante Antigüedades
Exuding European old-world elegance, enjoy the filet mignon and lobster as well as Cuban interpretations of international dishes, such as *bistec uruguayo* (see p56). ◈ *Map F2 • Av. 1ra & Calle 59, Varadero • (45) 66 7329 • $$$*

5 Restaurante La Fondue
Imported cheeses find their way into creative fondues, but squid in tomato sauce is also on the menu. ◈ *Map F2 • Av. 1ra & Calle 62, Varadero • (45) 66 7747 • $$$*

6 Restaurante Colibrí
A pleasant restaurant on the road to Zapata and Playa Larga. Crocodile dishes are a specialty. ◈ *Map F3 • Boca La Guamá • (45) 91 5662 • Closed for dinner • $$*

7 Restaurante 1869
A historic hotel furnished in period fashion. The creative menu here offers paella and a tasty calamari in tomato sauce. ◈ *Map G3 • Calle 31 & Av. 54, Cienfuegos • (43) 55 1020 • $$*

8 Palacio del Valle
The fare may be average, but the surroundings astound in this grandiose mansion in Mughal style. A pianist entertains in the evenings. ◈ *Map G3 • Calle 37 & Av. 0, Cienfuegos • (43) 55 1003 • $$$*

9 Restaurante El Farallón
Overhanging a gorgeous beach and turquoise waters, this simple, thatched restaurant serves great seafood; the garlic seabass is superb. ◈ *Map J1 • Villa Las Brujas, Cayo Santa María • (42) 35 0024 • $$*

10 Café Europa
One of few dining options in Santa Clara, this European-style café has a patio open to Santa Clara's main boulevard. Burgers, pizzas, and sandwiches are served, along with a local draft beer. ◈ *Map H3 • Av. Independencia & Calle Luis Estévez, Santa Clara • (42) 21 6350 • $*

> **Note:** Unless otherwise stated, all restaurants accept credit cards and serve vegetarian meals.

Left **View of Valle de Los Ingenios** Right **Tourists boating at Jardines del Rey**

Central Cuba East

FROM THE ATMOSPHERIC COLONIAL CITY OF *Trinidad to the gorgeous beaches of the Jardines del Rey, this region is one of the most exciting in Cuba. The terrain ranges from the sugar territory of the Valle de los Ingenios and the forested mountains around Topes de Collantes to the tourist-friendly spots in Cayo Coco and Cayo Guillermo. Trinidad, one of Cuba's most vibrant historic cities, is a wonderful base for exploring Topes and for scuba diving off the beach at nearby Playa Ancón. Camagüey is notable for its colonial architecture. The Carretera Central connects the key sites, but the wilderness of Jardines de la Reina is accessible solely by boat.*

Sunbathers at Playa Ancón

Sights

1. Sancti Spíritus
2. Trinidad
3. Valle de Los Ingenios
4. Gran Parque Natural Topes de Collantes
5. Jardines del Rey
6. Camagüey
7. Parque Nacional Jardines de la Reina
8. Playa Ancón
9. Playa Santa Lucía
10. Las Tunas

Preceding pages **Miniature 1950s American autos, Trinidad**

A street in Sancti Spíritus

Sancti Spíritus
Founded in 1522, this city is often overlooked by visitors, who tend to focus on neighboring Trinidad. The historic core of Sancti Spíritus has elegant mansions and brightly colored colonial homes graced by wrought-iron lanterns and grills. Sights include the Yayabo bridge and Parque Serafín Sánchez. The highlight is Plaza Honorato, with its Casa de la Trova and the Iglesia Parroquial Mayor del Espíritu Santo – a 17th-century church with a spectacular ceiling. ◈ Map J3 • Iglesia Parroquial Mayor del Espíritu Santo: Calle Agramonte Oeste 58, (41) 32 4855; adm

Trinidad
Cuba's most endearing colonial city was founded in 1514 by Diego Velázquez and named a UNESCO World Heritage Site in 1988. Closed to traffic, the cobbled streets have remained largely unchanged since the 18th century, when Trinidad grew wealthy from trade in slavery and sugar. The museums, churches, and plazas are intriguing, but the real joy is in wandering the narrow streets and observing daily life (see pp16–17).

Valle de Los Ingenios
A broad carpet of sugarcane covers this fertile vale northeast of Trinidad. The area gets its name from the many sugar mills (ingenios) built during the 18th and 19th centuries, when vast sugar plantations occupied the entire valley. While many of the sugar-cane estates are in the process of being restored as museums, the main house of the Hacienda Manaca Iznaga estate has been converted into a res-taurant. Climb its 147-ft (45-m) tower for a great view of the valley. ◈ Map H4 • Hacienda Manacas Iznaga: Iznaga; (41) 99 7241; adm

Gran Parque Natural Topes de Collantes
The steep drive to the northwest of Trinidad is well rewarded at Topes de Collantes, which functions as a base for hikes to towering waterfalls and the colonial-era coffee estate at Finca Codina, where caves and a beautiful orchid garden can be explored. Topes has many hotels in its vicinity, including the vast Kurhotel, which is dedicated to health tourism. Reserva y Coordinación oversees the arrangements for organized tours and guides. ◈ Map H4 • Reserva y Coordinación: Topes de Collantes; (42) 54 0117 • Kurhotel Escambray: (42) 54 0180

Antiguo Convento de San Francisco de Asis

Nuestra Señora de la Merced, Camagüey

5 Jardines del Rey

Off the north coast of Ciego de Ávila and Camagüey, the Jardines del Rey ("King's Garden") archipelago comprises about 400 islands, mostly uninhabited. Cayo Coco, one of the largest isles, and neighboring Cayo Guillermo have tourist hotels and watersports along the beaches. The diving is superb, and flamingos flock to the inshore lagoons *(see pp18–19)*.

6 Camagüey

Cuba's third largest city is replete with colonial and Neo-Classical buildings lining restored plazas. The city's network of streets – designed to thwart pirates – can be confusing to visitors. Sites include the Catedral Nuestra Señora de la Merced, museums and Teatro Principal – home to the Ballet de Camagüey. Two hotels complement the private room rentals. The city's nightlife is best experienced at the Casa de la Trova *(see p23)*.

La Trocha

A line of defence was built by the Spanish during the 19th-century Wars of Independence to block the advance of Cuban nationalist forces, the *mambises*. La Trocha stretched across Cuba from Morón, north of Ciego de Ávila, to Júcaro, on the Caribbean coast, and featured fortified towers.

7 Parque Nacional Jardines de la Reina

More than 600 deserted isles scattered on waters off Ciego de Ávila and Camagüey provinces form a marine Eden protected by a long coral reef. Marine turtles lay their eggs on beaches, while iguanas laze in the sun and flamingos wade in the shallows. Two cruise vessels and a floating hotel cater to anglers and divers. The Avalon Dive Center at Júcaro handles all visiting arrangements.
※ *Map J4 • Avalon Dive Center; (33) 49 8104; www.avalons.net*

8 Playa Ancón

The slender Península de Ancón south of Trinidad is lined by a fine, white-sand beach *(see p17)* served by three tourist hotels. With shallow waters good for swimming and snorkeling, it is also frequented by the locals.

Playa Los Cocos, near Playa Santa Lucia

The town hall of Las Tunas

A dive center arranges trips to Cayo Blanco to view the fabulous black coral formations. A marina rents out sailboats prior to arriving in Cuba. ✆ *Map H4*

9 Playa Santa Lucía

Proclaimed as a beach-lovers' paradise by the Cuban tourist board, this lonesome resort has a lovely beach and fantastic opportunities for diving and seeing sharks being hand fed. Horse-drawn carriages travel to nearby Playa Los Cocos, an even lovelier beach adjoining a ramshackle fishing village. Dining and entertainment are limited to the all-inclusive hotels. ✆ *Map M3*

10 Las Tunas

A provincial capital located between central and eastern Cuba, Las Tunas suffered during the Wars of Independence *(see p30)* when the town was razed by fire. Carretera Central, the nation's main highway running through the heart of this city, is lined with charming houses. Parque Vicente García, the main square, features the Museo Histórico Provincial, which traces the town's history. The local tradition of ceramic art thrives in Las Tunas. ✆ *Map M4 • Museo Histórico Provincial: Calle Francisco Verona & Colón; (31) 34 8201; open 8:30am–4:30pm Tue–Thu, 11am–7pm Fri & Sat, 8am–noon Sun; adm CUC$1*

A Day in Camagüey

Morning

🕐 A full day is barely enough to explore this historically significant town. Get an early start in the morning in **Parque Agramonte** *(see p20)* and catch a glimpse of the equestrian statue, the Cathedral, and the **Casa de la Trova** *(see p23)*. Exit the square by following Calle Cisneros south. After two blocks, turn right. The street brings you to **Plaza San Juan de Dios** *(see p20)*, surrounded by 18th-century houses. Explore the museum inside the Iglesia y Hospital San Juan de Dios, then follow Calle Matias west three blocks. Turn right onto Calle 24 de Febrero. After five blocks, cobbled **Plaza del Carmen** *(see p20)* opens to the northwest at the junction with Calle Martí, and has life-like sculptures scattered about. Lunch on *bolice mechado* (beef dish) at **La Campana de Toledo** *(see p103)*.

Afternoon

Retrace your steps to Calle Martí following it east to Parque Agramonte. Turn left onto Calle Cisneros to reach Plaza de los Trabajadores. On your right, **Casa Natal Ignacio Agramonte** *(see p21)* is worth a peek before exploring the **Catedral Nuestra Señora de la Merced** *(see p21)*. Don't miss the Santo Sepulcro – a silver sepulchre. Exit the square to the northwest and walk one block to the **Teatro Principal** *(see p21)* on your right. Then stroll north along Calle Enrique José to the **Museo Ignacio Agramonte** *(see p21)*. Continue south along Calle República to return to the town center.

Left **Casa de los Conspiradores** Center **Plazuela de Jigüe** Right **Palacio Cantero**

Colonial Trinidad

1 Plaza Mayor
Trinidad's main square is surrounded by 18th-century mansions. Two bronze grey-hounds on the south side are popular with kids *(see p16)*.

2 Palacio Brunet
Boasting marble floors, decorative tilework, and fan windows, this mansion is now the Museo Romántico featuring period furniture *(see p16)*.

3 Iglesia y Convento de San Francisco
Built in 1730 by Franciscan monks, this convent is currently home to the Museo de la Lucha Contra Bandidos. ⊗ *Calle Hernández Echerri 59 & Guinart • (41) 99 4121 • Open 9am–5pm Tue–Sun • Adm*

4 Plazuela de Jigüe
This plaza was named after the *jigüe* (acacia) tree beneath which Father Bartolomé de las Casas celebrated the city's first mass in 1514.

5 Iglesia Parroquial de la Santísima Trinidad
The Church of the Holy Trinity was built in 1892 on the site of the original parish church and has a Gothic altar. ⊗ *Plaza Mayor*

6 Palacio Cantero
Home to the Museo Histórico Municipal, this gem is filled with sumptuous period furnishings and eclectic exhibits on Trinidad's history *(see p16)*.

7 Casa de Aldemán Ortíz
This early 19th-century mansion has a balcony with views of the plaza and an art gallery. ⊗ *Calle Rubén Martínez Villena & Calle Bolívar • (41) 99 4432 • Open 8am–5pm Tue–Sat, 8am–1pm Sun & Mon*

8 Iglesia de Santa Ana
At the northeast corner of the old city, this semi-derelict church stands over a small plaza with a lively cultural center in a former prison. ⊗ *Calle Camilo Cienfuegos & Calle José Mendoza*

9 Ermita de Nuestra Señora de la Candelaria de la Popa
With a triple-arched bell tower, this tiny church is poised on a hill overlooking Trinidad. The chapel is closed but the views from here are worth the climb. ⊗ *Calle Simón Bolívar Final*

10 Casa de los Conspiradores
This intriguing home named for the nationalist conspirators that rendezvoused here is now an art gallery. ⊗ *Calle Hernández Echerrí & Rosario*

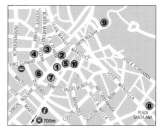

Left **Cayo Coco** Right **Pedraplén at Jardines del Rey**

🔟 The Cays

Cayo Coco
More than 14 miles (20 km) of gorgeous white beaches, crystal-clear turquoise ocean, and excellent all-inclusive hotels draw visitors from far and wide to Cayo Coco. ◈ *Map K2*

Cayo Guillermo
Linked to Cayo Coco by a narrow causeway, this small cay is similarly blessed with stunning beaches and warm waters. Its mangroves provide good opportunities for those interested in birding *(see p18).*

Cayo Sabinal
A remote cay that is accessible solely by a dirt road or by boat excursions from Playa Santa Lucía, Cayo Sabinal has three spectacular beaches, but facilities are scarce. Wild pigs roam the scrub-covered interior *(see p19).*

Diving with Sharks
Certified divers can experience thrilling encounters with sharks on organized dives at Cayo Coco and Playa Santa Lucía. In Jardines de la Reina, guides even ride the sharks.

Cayo Paredón Grande
This scrub-covered cay offers a beach with a superb bar and watersports that can be arranged through hotels. Built in 1859, the intriguing Faro Diego Velázquez lighthouse, is located here. ◈ *Map L2*

Pedraplén
This causeway connects Cayo Coco to the mainland. Made of solid earth with only two sluices, it bisects the existing bay and has an impeded tidal flow *(see p19).*

Cayo Romano
Spectacular coral reefs await visitors to this large uninhabited cay. A road connects to the mainland at Brasil, where a military checkpoint sometimes denies access. ◈ *Map L2*

Fishing
Fishing enthusiasts can follow the example of Ernest Hemingway who fished the waters off the Jardines de la Reina for marlin and other gamefish. Sport-fishing trips are offered from the main beach resorts at the cays and by Avalon Dive Center *(see p98).*

Centro de Investigaciones de Ecosistemas Costeros
This center for coastal environmental studies and protection is open to the public and features exhibits on manatees, flamingos, and coral reefs. ◈ *Map K2 • Cayo Coco • (33) 30 1161*

Cayo Anclitas
In the heart of the Jardines de la Reina, this tiny cay has a turtle farm and a visitors' center. A floating hotel offshore hosts diving and fishing excursions. ◈ *Map K2*

Left **Sierra Del Escambray mountains** Center **Playa Ancón** Right **Tropical forest in Sagüa-Baracoa**

Landscape Features

1 Mogotes
These dramatic limestone formations *(see p13)* add beauty to the pleasure of hiking in the Área Protegida de Recursos Manejados Sierra del Chorrillo, southeast of Camagüey. ⊗ *Map M4*

2 Sugarcane Fields
The southern half of the Sancti Spíritus province is a veritable sea of sugarcane extending east into much of Ciego de Ávila province. Feathery fronds rise from the stalks during the dry summer months.

3 Rugged Mountains
The craggy, thickly forested Alturas de Banao was a base for Che Guevara's guerrilla army in 1958. Trails lead from Campismo Planta Cantú, a holiday camp with cabins. ⊗ *Campismo Planta Cantú: Map J3 • Carretera Cacahual • (41) 329 698*

4 Plains
Hardy cattle munch the windswept, grassy plains of eastern Ciego de Ávila and Camagüey provinces, where the cowboy lifestyle is still very much alive.

5 Lakes
Anglers delight in the many fish species near Sancti Spíritus, and in the milky-colored Laguna de la Leche and Lago de Redonda, both outside Morón. ⊗ *Morón: Map K2*

6 Coral Cays
Enhanced by their jewel-like settings in seas of jade and aquamarine, hundreds of coral cays speckle the oceans off Central Cuba East. Most are uninhabited but offer excellent wildlife viewing.

7 Tropical Forest
Dense montane forests cloak much of this region. Sierra del Chorrillo, south of Camagüey, is an excellent venue for those who want to explore the tropical dry forests. ⊗ *Map L4*

8 Underground Caves
Caves make up a large part of the limestone uplands around Topes de Collantes *(see p46)*. The Cueva del Jabalí at Cayo Coco *(see p101)* features a restaurant and cabaret.

9 Waterfalls
Drenched in rainfall, the Sierra del Escambray around Topes de Collantes *(see p46)* resounds to the thunderous noise of cascades splashing into crystal-clear pool. The Salto de Caburní is easily reached by a well-trodden trail.

10 Beaches
Sandy beaches unfurl along the Atlantic shore of the Jardines del Rey *(see pp18–19)*. The cays of the Jardines de la Reina *(see p98)* are also ringed by white sands. The mainland shore has few beaches *(see pp48–9)*.

Restaurante Iberostar

Price Categories

For a three-course meal with half a bottle of wine or equivalent including taxes and extra charges.

$	under CUC$100
$$	CUC$100–175
$$$	CUC$175–250
$$$$	CUC$250–325
$$$$$	over CUC$325

🔟 Restaurants

1 Mesón de la Plaza
Re-creating the ambience of a Spanish *bodega* with cowhide chairs and benches, this restaurant serves bargain-priced dishes. ✪ *Map J2 • Calle Máximo Gómez 34, Sancti Spíritus • (41) 32 8546 • $$*

2 Paladar Estela
One of Cuba's finest regional *paladares* (small, private restaurants), Paladar Estela offers courtyard dining. Try the excellent marinated braised lamb. ✪ *Map H4 • Calle Bolívar 557, Trinidad • (41) 99 4329 • Open Mon–Fri dinner only • $$$$$*

3 Restaurante Santa Ana
Ropa vieja (see p56) is a culinary highlight at this eatery, housed in a former prison. Troubadors entertain with traditional songs. ✪ *Map H4 • Calle Camilo Cienfuegos & Rúben Batista, Trinidad • (41) 99 6423 • $$$$$*

4 Restaurante Iberostar
A fantastically plush option inside the Iberostar Gran Hotel Trinidad. International dishes are prepared with aplomb. ✪ *Map H4 • Calle José Martí 262, Trinidad • (41) 99 6073 • $$$$$*

5 Restaurante Manacas Iznaga
This former sugar-estate owner's mansion provides a unique setting for enjoying traditional Cuban dishes. ✪ *Map H4 • Iznaga, Valle de los Ingenios • (41) 99 7241 • $$$$$*

6 Restaurante Solaris
This elegant restaurant offers a bird's-eye view over central Ciego de Ávila. A pianist creates a romantic mood, and a dress code applies. ✪ *Map K3 • Calle Honorato del Castillo & Libertad, Ciego de Ávila • (33) 22 2156 • $$$$$*

7 Restaurante Santa María
Camagüey's best eatery combines elegant period decor with a wide-ranging menu. ✪ *Map L3 • Hotel Colón, Calle República 472, Camagüey • (32) 28 3346 • $$$$$*

8 Gran Hotel
Of the Gran Hotel's two eateries, the rooftop restaurant is preferred for its quality buffet dinner. The fine views over the city center are a definite bonus. ✪ *Map L3 • Calle Maceo 67, Camagüey • (32) 29 2093 • $$$$$*

9 La Campana de Toledo
Located in the center of Camagüey, opposite one of the most emblematic plazas in the town, the specialty here is *bolice mechado*, a local beef delicacy. ✪ *Map L3 • Plaza San Juan de Dios, Camagüey • (32) 28 6812 • $$*

10 El Baturro
Part of a growing national chain, this restaurant in a historic beamed mansion has a delight-fully cozy ambience. The paella and shrimp enchilada are tasty and filling. ✪ *Map M4 • Calle Vicente García between Santana & Ortuño, Las Tunas • (31) 37 1523 • $$$$$*

Unless otherwise stated, all restaurants accept credit cards, serve vegetarian meals, and are open for lunch and dinner.

Left **Sitio Histórico Birán** Right **Visitors climbing the Loma de la Cruz steps in Holguín**

The Far East

FORMERLY KNOWN AS ORIENTE, *far-eastern Cuba is dominated by rugged mountains. The Sierra Maestra was the major base of Fidel Castro's guerrilla army (see p34), and the Sierra Cristal and Sierra Purial comprise a wilderness of mountain rain forest and offer spectacular hiking and birding. The coastline is no less rugged with lovely beaches lining the shore of Holguín. Historic cities dot this corner of the republic; Santiago de Cuba – birthplace of the Revolution (see pp24–25) – teems with sites of cultural note while Baracoa is the country's oldest city. Cuba's African heritage is keenly felt in Santiago de Cuba and Guantánamo, the birthplaces of son and changüí (see pp42–3) respectively.*

The clear turquoise sea at Playa Guardalavaca

🔟 Sights

1. Santiago de Cuba
2. Holguín
3. Gibara
4. Playa Guardalavaca
5. Museo Aborigen Chorro de Maíta
6. Sitio Histórico Birán
7. Zoológico de Piedra
8. Bayamo
9. El Cobre
10. Baracoa

Preceding pages **Leisurely games of chess, Santiago de Cuba**

A fortress at Santiago de Cuba

Santiago de Cuba
Graced by intriguing buildings, this sprawling industrial city was Cuba's capital until 1553, Santiago de Cuba's colonial core *(casco histórico)*. Must-see sites include the Cathedral, Casa-Museo de Diego Velázquez, the Museo Emilio Bacardí, and the Moncada barracks – the base for Castro's revolution in 1953 *(see pp30 – 31)*. Following the Haitian revolution in 1791, French and Haitian migrants flooded the city and fostered unique forms of architecture, music, and dance. Don't miss the annual Festival del Pregón in July *(see p53)*.
✪ *Casa Museo de Diego Velázquez: Calle Félix Pena 612; (22) 65 2652, 9am–12:45pm, 2–4:45pm Mon–Thu & Sat; 2–4:45pm Fri; 9am–12:45pm Sun; adm*

Holguín
This industrious provincial capital featuring colonial plazas, several churches, and museums is worth exploring. Its most famous son is Calixto García, a general in the Wars of Independence *(see p30)*. His house, now containing a museum, stands near Plaza Calixto García, where the Museo Provincial de Historia displays period pieces. Climb the steps to the top of Loma de la Cruz for splendid views. Mirador de Mayabe offers a grand mountain-top lunch *(see pp22–3)*.

Gibara
Once a wealthy port town, Gibara now draws much of its current income from a fishing fleet that harbors in picturesque Bahía de Bariay. The original city walls are now relics, but Parque Calixto García boasts a colonial church and museums of natural history and decorative arts. The town's white-painted houses lend the city its nickname, "Villa Blanca" (White City). Many colonial homes offer private room rentals *(see p23)*.

Playa Guardalavaca
This beach zone an hour's drive north of Holguín was developed as a holiday resort in the mid-1980s and is now Cuba's third-largest resort destination. Current development is focused on the white-sand beaches of Esmeralda *(see p49)*, Yuraguanal, and Pesquero, and either side of flask-shaped Bahía de Naranjo. The bay has an aquarium with dolphin shows, while trails provide insights into local ecology *(see p23)*.

Gibara's colonial church

Columbus in Cuba

Inhabitants of Baracoa believe that Christopher Columbus landed in the Bahía de Miel and that the flat-topped mountain he described was El Yunque *(see p27)*. Experts, however, believe that the mountain was the Silla de Gibara and that Columbus actually landed in the Bahía de Bariay on October 28, 1492.

Museo Aborigen Chorro de Maíta

This archaeological site is one of the largest native Indian burial sites in the Caribbean. Of the 108 skeletons unearthed, many still lie in situ as they were found, and can be seen from a boardwalk. A museum displays pottery and other artifacts. The neighboring Aldea Taína re-creates an Indian village with life-size statues and the locals re-enact Taíno life. ◊ Map P4 • *5 miles (8 km) east of Guardalavaca* • *(24) 43 0201 • Open 9am–5pm Tue–Sun, 9am–1pm Mon • Adm for Aldea Taína*

Sitio Histórico Birán

Opened to the public in 2002, the Finca Manacas estate, outside Birán, where Fidel Castro was born and lived until his adolescence, belonged to his father Angel Castro *(see p34)*. The wooden mansion has been restored and is furnished with original family pieces. The grounds include Fidel's parents' graves, a former schoolhouse, and buildings, which were relocated to create an idealized village. Guided tours are available. ◊ Map N4 • *(24) 28 6114 • Open 8am–4pm Tue–Sun • Adm*

Zoológico de Piedra

Referred to as a "stone zoo" for more than 400 life-size animals that are displayed here. The animals, including lions, an elephant, a gorilla, and crocodiles are carved from stone by coffee farmer Angel Iñigo. He is a self-taught sculptor who used photographs to hew the creatures. Iñigo has also created entire vignettes such as monkeys picking fleas and Taíno Indians killing a wild boar. A restaurant serves *criollo* meals. ◊ Map Q5 • *Boquerón de Yateras • Open 8am–5pm daily • Adm*

A stone ape at Zoológico de Piedra

Bayamo

Founded in 1513 by Diego Velásquez, Bayamo is Cuba's second oldest city. In the early 19th century it was the cradle of revolt against Spanish rule. Much of the original city was destroyed in 1869 when citizens razed their town rather than surrender to the invading Spanish forces. Fortunately, many key sites survived this destruction and today the restored historic core is a national monument. Most sights are concentrated around Parque Céspedes and Plaza del Himno, including the not-to-be-missed Parroquial Mayor de San Salvador

View of Baracoa and El Yunque

Nuestra Señora del Cobre, El Cobre

church and the Casa Natal de Carlos Manuel de Céspedes.
◈ *Map N5 • Parroquial Mayor de San Salvador: (23) 42 2514; open Mon–Fri 9am–noon & 3–5pm, Sat 9am–noon; adm • Casa Natal de Carlos Manuel de Céspedes: (23) 42 3864; open Tue–Fri. 10am–6pm, Sat 10am–2:30pm 8pm–10pm, Sun 10am–3pm; adm*

9 El Cobre

This village is named after the copper *(cobre)* mined here in early colonial days. Today it is famous for the Basílica de Nuestra Señora del Cobre *(see p25),* built in 1926 on a hill over-looking the town. Many pilgrims arrive here to beseech favors of the statue of Virgen de la Caridad del Cobre, and leave offerings in the Sala de Milagros (Salon of Miracles). ◈ *Map P6 • 12 miles (20 km) northwest of Santiago • (22) 34 6118 • Sala de Milagros: open 6:30am–6pm*

10 Baracoa

Cuba's most easterly city, Baracoa *(see pp26–7)* is spec-tacularly set within a broad bay. The El Castillo hotel *(see p27),* a former fortress, provides the best views in town. The city has a church with a cross that locals believe was brought over by Columbus. Baracoa is a good base for hiking and birdwatching, especially at Parque Nacional Alejandro Humboldt *(see p47).*

A Drive from Santiago to Baracoa

Morning

Leave early from **Santiago de Cuba** *(see p107),* tak-ing the Autopista Nacional, which begins in the Vista Alegre district. Be careful on the freeway, which has plenty of potholes and stray traffic. After about 5 miles (8 km), exit at the signed junction for La Maya. The road passes through sugarcane fields, with the Sierra Baconao rising to the south. Conti-nue east to Guantánamo, where sites of interest around Parque Martí can be explored in one hour. Crossing the Río Bano, divert north to Boquerón de Yateras to reach the **Zoológico de Piedra,** and lunch at the restaurant.

Afternoon

Return to Guantánamo and turn east for Baracoa. The road passes the entrance to Mirador de Malones and meets the shore at Playa Yateritas. At Cajobabo, turn south to reach Playitas, where a museum recalls José Martí's return from exile. Visit the memorial at the spot where Martí landed with General Máximo Gómez *(see p31).* Beyond Cajobabo, the road snakes into the Sierra de Purial via **La Farola** *(see p112).* The mountain road is scenic but drive carefully, espe-cially in fog and rain. At the summit, Alto de Coltillo, have a hot coffee from the roadside shacks before winding down the mountain's north side toward a coastal plain. Before reaching Baracoa, stop at the small zoo, Parque Zoológico Cacique Guamá (open 9am–5pm Tue–Sun).

Left **Playa Siboney** Center **Valle de la Prehistoria** Right **Prado de las Esculturas**

Parque Baconao Sites

1 Playa Siboney
This pebbly beach frequented by locals has *casas particulares* with rooms overlooking the Caribbean *(see p49)*.

2 Valle de la Prehistoria
Life-sized model dinosaurs cast in concrete and steel are found at this park *(see p44)*. ◈ Map P6 • Carretera de Baconao, km 6.5 • (22) 39 9239 • Open 8am–4:45pm • Adm

3 Ave del Paraíso
Cubanacán offers tours to visit this elevated garden, with flowers that bloom all year round. ◈ Map P6 • Viajes Cubanacán: Av. de las Américas & M, Santiago • (22) 64 2202 • Open 7am–4pm • Adm

4 Museo de Automóviles
Among the cars on display is the curious one-cylinder Maya Cuba. An adjoining museum has 2,500 toy cars. ◈ Map P6 • Conjunto de Museos de la Punta, Carretera de Baconao • (22) 39 9197 • Open 8am–5pm • Adm

5 Cafetal La Isabelica
Learn about coffee production at this 18th-century coffee estate. ◈ Map P6 • Carretera de la Gran Piedra, km 14 • Open 8am–4pm • Adm

6 Prado de las Esculturas
A trail leads past metal artworks in this sculpture garden. ◈ Map P6 • Carretera a Siboney & Carretera de la Gran Piedra • Open 8am–4pm • Adm

7 Museo de la Guerra Hispano-Cubano-Americana
This museum exhibits original weaponry and uniforms from the 1898 Spanish-American War *(see p37)*. ◈ Map P6 • Carretera Siboney, km 13 • (22) 39 9119 • Open 9am–5pm Mon–Sat • Adm

8 Comunidad Artística Los Mamoncillos
Shop for ceramics and other original art pieces produced at this tiny hamlet dedicated to arts and crafts. Most artists welcome visitors to their studios. ◈ Map Q1 • Playa Verraco, Carretera de Baconao

9 Acuario Baconao
This aquatic park displays sharks, marine turtles, and other sea-life in tanks. Dolphin shows are held twice daily. ◈ Map Q6 • Carretera de Baconao, km 47 • (22) 35 6156 • Open 9am–5pm Tue–Sun • Adm

10 Laguna Baconao
This lake enfolded by mountains is inhabited by crocodiles, also bred at a facility at Complejo Turístico, from where boat trips are offered. ◈ Map Q6 • Complejo Turístico • (22) 35 0004 • Open 8am–5pm

Left **Sea view from Parque Nacional Desembarco del Granma** Right **A steam train**

🔟 Things to Do

1 Hiking in Parque Nacional Desembarco del Granma
The site of the *Granma* landing *(see p32)*, this park features trails through semi-arid forest with caves. The marine terraces offer great views *(see p47)*.

2 Dive at Marea del Portillo
This otherwise modest beach resort will thrill scuba aficionados with its splendid dive sites. The highlight is the wreck of the Spanish warship, *Cristóbal Colón*, which was sunk in 1898. 🖎 *Map M6 • Albacora Dive Center: Marea del Portillo; (23) 59 7139*

3 Drive to Chivirico
Soaring skyward from a teal-blue sea, the Sierra Maestra push up against a barren coast road linking Marea del Portillo with Santiago de Cuba. The stunning scenery can distract you from the road. 🖎 *Map M6–P6*

4 Dance at the Casa de la Trova, Santiago
The epicenter of *son* music *(see p42)*, Casa de la Trova has been a center of learning for renowned musicians. Paintings of famous artists adorn the walls.

5 Honor José Martí at Dos Ríos
The site of José Martí's martyr-dom *(see p31)* is marked by an obelisk. The memorial, surrounded by white roses, is an allusion to Martí's famous poem, *Cultivo una rosa blanca*. 🖎 *Map N5*

6 Watch the sunrise at Punta Maisí
Clamber the stairs of the lighthouse to watch the sunrise at Cuba's easternmost point. A 4WD vehicle is recommended to get there. 🖎 *Map R5*

7 Boat ride at Yumurí
The Río Yumurí runs through coastal mountains and is a stunning setting for boat trips departing from the wharf at the river mouth. Negotiate a fee with the boat owners. 🖎 *Map R5*

8 Spot manatees at Parque Nacional Alejandro Humboldt
Guided boat trips arranged through Gaviotatours offer the chance for a rare encounter with the endearing and endangered manatees as they paddle around in the mangrove-lined waters of Parque Natural Bahía de Taco. 🖎 *Gaviotatours: Hotel Castillo, Baracoa; (21) 64 5165*

9 Birding in Sierra Cristal
Sightings of Cuban parrots and tocororos *(see pp50–51)* are the rewards for bird enthusiasts on hikes through the montane forests of northeastern Cuba.

10 Steam train ride
Hop onto an antique steam train at Rafael Freyre for a scenic tour of the Grupo Maniabón mountains *(see p112)*. Tours can be arranged through hotel desks in Guardalavaca and Holguín.

Left **Stunning views from La Farola** Right **A bird of paradise at Gran Piedra's botanical garden**

Mountain Highs

1 La Farola
Experience a winding, breathtakingly steep drive up the mountain connecting Guantánamo to Baracoa. Magnificent scenery awaits drivers, but extreme care is required on the way up. ⬊ *Map R5*

2 El Yunque
With a unique flat-topped shape that forms a dramatic backdrop to Baracoa, you can drive or hike to the summit. The views from the top are fabulous and worth the trip *(see p27)*.

3 Parque Nacional Alejandro Humboldt
Don sturdy footwear for the hike into the mountains of this park, which features *miradores* (look-outs) offering fine views. Guides are mandatory and Gaviotatours can arrange them for you. ⬊ *Map R5 • Gaviotatours: Hotel Castillo, Baracoa; (21) 64 5165*

4 El Saltón
This ecotourism mountain resort offers trails, waterfalls, and superb birding. The Hotel El Saltón is a good base for exploring. ⬊ *Map N5 • Hotel El Saltón: (22) 56 6326*

5 Pinares de Mayarí
Accessed by a daunting dirt road, this mountain resort *(see p47)* formerly served the Communist Party elite. Enjoy outdoor activities amid the pine forests. ⬊ *Map P5 • (24) 50 3308*

6 Parque Nacional Pico Turquino
Cuba's highest peak *(see p47)* is a challenging two-day ascent leading through various eco-systems, including a cloud forest. ⬊ *Map N6*

7 Grupo Maniabón
Surrounded by *mogotes (see p102)*, this visually delightful mountain chain northeast of Holguín is best explored via a steam train excursion. ⬊ *Map P4*

8 La Comandancia de la Plata
Fidel Castro's former guerrilla headquarters, deep in the Sierra Maestra and hidden by thick forest, are kept as they were five decades ago, with Fidel's own hut overhanging a ravine *(see p33)*.

9 Gran Piedra
This "Great Stone" is a massive boulder balanced atop the ridge-crest of the Sierra Baconao which is reached via a 454-step staircase. It offers pano-ramic views over Santiago de Cuba and has a botanical garden. ⬊ *Map P6*

10 Mayarí Arriba
The Museo Comandancia del Segundo Frente recalls the years of the Revolution when the pine forests surrounding this town were the setting for guerrilla war-fare. ⬊ *Map P5 • Museo Comandancia del Segundo Frente: Av. de los Mártires; (22) 42 5749; open 8am–4pm daily; adm*

Price Categories

For a three-course	**$** under CUC$100
meal with half a bottle	**$$** CUC$100–175
of wine or equivalent	**$$$** CUC$175–250
including taxes and	**$$$$** CUC$250–325
extra charges.	**$$$$$** over CUC$325

Left **Restaurante Casa Granda**

Restaurants

Restaurante Casa Granda
This classy restaurant in the Hotel Casa Granda has elegant, old-fashioned decor, and a menu that features satisfying *criollo* and continental fare. ✪ *Map P6 • Calle Heredia 201, Santiago de Cuba • (22) 65 3023 (ext. 522) • $$$*

Restaurante El Morro
This delightfully rustic restaurant sits atop a coastal headland. Eat your meal while enjoying the spectacular views from the terrace. ✪ *Map P6 • Parque Histórico El Morro, Santiago de Cuba • (22) 69 1576 • $$*

Restaurante 1720
Located in a restored colonial mansion, Restaurante 1720 offers a creative menu that includes *paella*, and a tasty creole shrimp in rum. ✪ *Map N4 • Calle Frexes 190, Holguín • (24) 46 8150 • $$$*

Restaurante Loma de la Cruz
Incomparable views over the city are offered at the Spanish-*bodega*-style Loma de la Cruz. Be sure to try the tasty lamb *enchilada*. ✪ *Map N4 • Loma de la Cruz, Holguín • (24) 46 4821 • $$*

Restaurante La Habanera
A small, clean, and charming place in the Hotel La Habanera, this restaurant specializes in fish filet with garlic and herbs. ✪ *Map R5 • Calle Maceo 126, Baracoa • (21) 64 5273 • Open 7am–10pm • $$*

Taberna Pancho
Join the locals for hearty set meals of shrimp and pork that can be washed down with draft beer at Taberna Pancho. ✪ *Map N4 • Av. Dimitrov, Holguín • (24) 48 1868 • $*

El Ancla
A seafood restaurant beside the shore, El Ancla's fish dishes are value for money, but the lobster is expensive. ✪ *Map P4 • Playa Mayor, Guardalavaca • (24) 43 0381 • $$$$*

La Sevillana
The best restaurant in town, La Sevillana serves Spanish and *criollo* dishes. The restaurant offers two seatings daily. ✪ *Map N5 • General García between Figueredo and Lora, Bayamo • (23) 42 1472 • Open noon–2pm, 6–10pm, closed Tue • $$*

Restaurante Zunzún
This atmospheric eatery has a wide-ranging menu. Housed in a colonial mansion, enjoy your meal in the comfort of the air-conditioned indoors or be seated at the terrace outside. ✪ *Map P6 • Av. Manduley 159, Santiago de Cuba • (22) 64 1528 • Open noon–10pm • $$$*

Restaurante Duaba
This modestly elegant air-conditioned restaurant offers unexpectedly creative dishes, such as *gouda* aubergine. ✪ *Map R5 • Hotel El Castillo, Baracoa • (21) 64 5165 • Open 7–9:45am, noon–3pm, 7–10pm • $$$*

Unless otherwise stated, all restaurants accept credit cards and serve vegetarian meals.

STREETSMART

CUBA'S TOP 10

Left **Opening times** Center **Women wearing sun hats** Right **Customs regulated Cuban rum**

Planning Your Trip

1 Passports & Visa

All visitors must have a valid passport, a tourist card (see p117), and an onward ticket. It is wise to photocopy passport details in case of theft or loss. US law prohibits most of its citizens from visiting Cuba; those individuals permitted travel visas require a special license from the US Treasury Department.
⊛ US Treasury Department
• (202) 622 2000 • www. treas.gov/ofac

2 Customs Regulations

Visitors are allowed to bring in 200 cigarettes and 6 pints (3 liters) of spirits duty free, plus 44 lb (20 kg) of personal belongings. Laptop computers must be declared upon arrival, and certain electronic items are prohibited. Customs searches in Cuba can be rigorous, and the authorities take a harsh line on drugs.

3 Time Zone

Cuba is on Eastern Standard Time (EST) and is 5 hours behind Greenwich Mean Time (GMT), the same as New York and Miami. Daylight savings operate from May to October.

4 Insurance

Medical insurance is wise when visiting Cuba, as any illness or accident may involve paying for treatment. It is also worth having insurance against loss or theft of valuables. Visitors intending to engage in extreme sports should ensure that they are covered.

5 When to Go

Cuba's tourist season runs from December to April, when airfares, accommodations, and car rentals are at their dearest. This period is less hot than the rest of the year, but temperatures in January can reach 78°F (26°C). The hurricane season lasts from June to November, with the majority of storms occurring from August onwards.

6 What to Take

Light cotton clothing is recommended. Carry swimwear for a beach holiday, as such apparel can be expensive in Cuba. It is worth packing a sweater or lightweight jacket for heavily air-conditioned restaurants, chilly winter nights, and visits to mountainous regions. Long-sleeved clothing and mosquito repellent help guard against mosquitoes and sunscreen, hats, and sunglasses help to prevent sun damage.

7 How Long to Stay

Most visitors to Cuba arrive for beach vacations of a week to 10 days. Havana itself requires at least four days to fully explore, while Viñales, Trinidad, and Santiago de Cuba deserve two each. Allow at least three weeks to explore the length of Cuba, from Pinar del Río to Baracoa.

8 Electricity

Cuba's erratic electricity supply works on a 110-volt system, as in the US and Canada, although some outlets are 220-volt and are usually marked. Plugs are the two-pin North American type, so European visitors may need adaptors. While power cuts are common, tourist facilities have private generators.

9 Insect Repellent

One of the most vital things to bring with you, repellent should be applied liberally on exposed skin, particularly at beach resorts and at night. Avoiding mosquito bites is essential when in Cuba, which has had recent dengue outbreaks.

10 Opening Hours

Most offices are open between 8:30am–12:30pm and 1:30am–5:30pm, Monday to Friday. Shops usually stay open 8:30am–5:30pm Monday to Saturday. Banks typically open 8:30am–noon and 1:30–3pm Monday to Friday, and 8:30–10:30am on Saturdays. Museum hours vary widely, although many are closed on Mondays.

Left **Yachts at the Hemingway marina** Right **A Cubana airplane**

Getting to Cuba

Airlines
Virgin Atlantic offers regular flights between London and Havana. Air France, Iberia, and KLM fly from Europe to Cuba, as do charter companies such as Air Europe, Martinair, LTU, and Monarch. Air Canada, Cubana, and many charter companies connect Canada with the island. No US companies fly to Cuba other than charter companies for licensed travelers only.

Air Fares
Fares are lower off-season from May to November and for mid-week departures. As far as possible, book in advance. Charter companies are usually cheaper than scheduled airlines, although more restrictions apply.

José Martí International Airport
Situated on the southern outskirts of Havana, Aeropuerto Internacional José Martí is the main entrance for visitors not arriving for a beach vacation. There is no bus service and travelers will need to take a taxi for the 40-minute ride into the city. The fare should cost about CUC\$15–25.

Santiago de Cuba Airport
The Aeropuerto Internacional Antonio Maceo is about 5 miles (8 km) south of Santiago de Cuba's center. Bus services are untrustworthy and unreliable, and the best bet is to take a taxi. Official tourist taxis should cost about CUC\$8–10, which you must agree upon with the driver in advance.

Other Airports
International airports are at Varadero, Ciego de Ávila, Cayo Coco, Camagüey (used for Playa Santa Lucía), and Holguín (primarily for the resorts of Guardalavaca), and Cayo Largo.

Tourist Cards
All visitors must present a tourist card at Cuban immigration upon arrival. The card costs CUC\$25 and is valid for 30 days; Canadians receive one for 90 days. Cards are issued upon checking in for your flight to Cuba and must be filled in before passing through passport control.

Airport Taxis
Tourist taxis are present at international airports. As few taxi drivers use meters, it is wise to agree upon a fare before setting off. Touts may attempt to steer you toward private taxis, but always decline the offer.

Changing Money at the Airport
It is impossible to obtain Cuban Convertible Pesos (see p120) outside Cuba, so exchange currency at the airport. Cadeca (see p120) offers money-changing services at the main airports.

Arriving by Ship
A few Caribbean-based cruise lines include Cuba in their itineraries, stopping at the port facilities in Havana and, less frequently, Santiago de Cuba and Cienfuegos.

Ports of Entry
Marinas around the island act as official ports of entry for independent sailors. However, US sailors require prior approval from the Coast Guard and Office of Foreign Assets Control.

International Airports

José Martí
Havana • *(7) 266 4133*

Antonio Maceo
Santiago de Cuba
• *(22) 69 8614*

Juan Gualberto Gómez
Varadero
• *(45) 24 7015*

Máximo Gómez
Ciego de Ávila
• *(33) 26 6003*

Cayo Coco
(33) 30 9161

Ignacio Agramonte
Camagüey
• *(32) 26 1010*

Frank País
Holguín • *(24) 46 2512*

Left **Classic car for rent** Center **The unique cocotaxi** Right **A bicitaxi moving through city streets**

TOP 10 Getting Around

1 Internal Flights
Cubana de Aviación has regular connections between Havana, the provincial capitals, and key tourist centers. Although it can be useful, demand exceeds supply and service is unreliable. Aerocaribbean also offers good service.

2 Long-Distance Buses
A good value and reliable bus service is provided by Viazul. It connects Havana to provincial capitals and some major tourist destinations. The buses are air-conditioned with toilets and comfortable seats. Astro provides a less reliable, slightly cheaper, but packed service; modern buses are being introduced.

3 Guaguas and Metrobuses
An inexpensive alternative to tourist buses, *guaguas* are local buses that are usually full to the brim with passengers. Metrobuses have replaced *camellos* (camels), the uncomfortable articulated buses that were pulled by lorries.

4 Car Rentals
Car rental is widely available, but expensive. All rental agencies are government owned. Contracts are required for all rentals and customer service is often lax. Rex is the most

reputable company of the pack but also the least cost effective.

5 Driving Conditions and Road Rules
Driving can be challenging due to poor roads, a lack of signs, and numerous obstacles. Poor lighting makes driving at night hazardous. *Tránsito* (traffic police) enforce speed limits of 30 mph (50 km/h) in towns, 37 mph (60 km/h) on rural roads, 55 mph (90 km/h) on highways, and 62 mph (100 km/h) on freeways.

6 Taxis
There is no shortage of taxis in main tourist areas. However, many drivers don't use their meters and will negotiate a fare. Cocotaxis are a unique mode of transportation. These egg-shaped, bright yellow scooters cost the same as a regular taxi and work particularly well for short distances.

7 Bicitaxis
These crude bicycle-rickshaws are a staple means of getting around within cities. Most are licensed to carry Cubans only. Those that can take tourists provide a fun, but uncomfortable, way to travel short distances.

8 Horse-and-Cart
Antique horse-drawn carriages are a good way of sightseeing in Old Havana, Varadero, and a

few other cities. For Cubans, rickety carts are the main means of getting around urban areas.

9 Camiones
These 1950s-era lorries make up for the inadequate bus service. They operate on a scheduled, albeit unreliable, service. They are perennially crowded and uncomfortable.

10 Walking
Cuba's colonial city centers are perfect for exploring on foot. Licensed guides can be hired in Old Havana, Trinidad, and Santiago de Cuba. Beware of hustlers on the street – they cannot be trusted. Be sure to wear comfortable shoes.

Local Airlines

Cubana de Aviación
Calle 23 & O, Havana
• *(7) 834 4449*
• *www.cubana.cu*

Aerocaribbean
Calle 23 No.64, Havana
• *(7) 879 7524 • www.
aero-caribbean.com*

Car Rentals

Rex
*(7) 683 0303 • www.
rex-rentacar.com*

Bus Services

Viazul
(7) 881 1413
• *www.viazul.cu*

Astro
(7) 870 3397

Left **Books about the Revolution** Center **A local tourist office** Right **A copy of the** *Granma*

🔟 Sources of Information

1 Tourist Offices Abroad

Official Cuban tourist offices in Canada and the United Kingdom provide basic information. For more specific details, it is better to contact independent agencies. US travelers should contact the Cubatur office in Canada.

2 Local Tourist Offices

Tourist offices are scattered throughout major tourist centers, but few have the resources to answer more than the most basic questions. Most are set up primarily to sell organized trips.

3 Websites

The Internet has a huge amount of information available. Cuban websites are all state-run and care should be taken if booking online. US websites are barred from accepting bookings for trips to Cuba.

4 English-Language News

The government's official newspaper, *Granma*, is published in English and distributed at tourist hotels. Most tourist hotels have satellite TV showing CNN and selected English-language news stations.

5 Local Publications

All media in Cuba is government-controlled. Publications are limited to *Granma*, a few other almost identical newspapers, and about half a dozen publications specializing in the arts. In Havana, the weekly *Cartelera* provides information on arts and culture in English.

6 Local Tour Operators

Cuba's larger tour operators can provide information on specific regions and activities, but their knowledge is often limited and unreliable. It is better to seek out smaller operators who can offer more specialized tours.

7 Maps

There are several good maps of the country; the best is by International Travel Maps. In Cuba, tourist outlets sell a tourist map of Havana published by Ediciones Geo, and *Guía de Carreteras*, an excellent road atlas. The best source for maps is El Navegante, situated in Old Havana.

8 Bookstores

A few bookstores in Havana and some shops in large tourist hotels sell a limited range of maps, books, and other travel-related literature. There are very few outlets elsewhere. A second-hand book sale is held on Havana's Plaza de Armas *(see p8)*, from Wednesday to Saturday.

9 Guides

Government-run tour operators can provide guides, and many taxi drivers also act as driver-guides. Car rental agencies will provide a driver-guide on request. Many individuals offer illegal freelance services, but caution must be taken when hiring them.

10 Libraries

Cuba has relatively few libraries *(bibliotecas)*, and the range of books is limited to works deemed politically correct. Havana's Biblioteca Nacional is restricted for both Cubans and foreigners, who must be sponsored by a Cuban government institution.

Local Tour Operators

Cubanacán Viajes
(7) 833 4090
• www.cubanacan.cu

Havanatur
(7) 830 8227
• www.havanatur.cu

Gaviotatours
(7) 204 7683
• www.gaviota-grupo.cu

Maps and Book Stores

Instituto Cubano del Libro
Calle O'Reilly 4, Habana Vieja • (7) 861 8585

Tienda El Navegante
Calle Mercaderes 115, Habana Vieja
• (7) 861 3625

Left **Cadeca sign** Center **The exterior of a post office** Right **A public telephone**

TOP 10 Banking and Communications

1 The Peso
The Cuban peso is made of 100 *centavos*. The peso is used mostly by Cubans; there are very few items that tourists will be able, or wish, to use pesos for except local buses, baseball stadiums, and food stalls on the street.

2 The Convertible Peso
All tourist transactions and major purchases are conducted in Cuban Convertible Pesos *(pesos convertibles)*, designated as CUC$, with notes of 1, 3, 5, 10, 20, 50, and 100. The value is pegged at US$1.08. However, it has no value outside Cuba. Euros can be used for transactions in Varadero, Cayo Coco, and Cayo Largo.

3 Banks and ATMs
All banks in Cuba are state-owned. Most will exchange foreign currency at the official rate, though queuing at the counter can be quite a lengthy operation. The regular opening hours are normally 8am–3pm Monday to Saturday, but 8am–noon on the last working day of each month. Some ATMs in major towns can be used to obtain cash advances using cards such as MasterCard and Visa, except for those that have been issued or processed by any US institutions.

4 Cadeca
Foreign currency can be exchanged for CUC$ and pesos at Cadeca *casas de cambio* (bureaux de change), found throughout the country. An 11 per cent commission is charged if you would like to change US dollars; however, no such commissions exist for other currencies.

5 Credit Cards
MasterCard and Visa are widely accepted in hotels, restaurants, and tourist-oriented stores, but not in out-of-the-way places and smaller outlets. Cards issued by US banks cannot be used. Be prepared for the electronic processing system to be unreliable and frequently not even functioning. Credit cards can be used in order to obtain cash advances at certain banks. An 11 per cent commission is charged for the usage of credit cards.

6 Telephones
Operated by ETECSA, a state company, public phones are plentiful and normally reliable. The system consists of public phones that work with prepaid phone cards for between CUC$5 and CUC$50. These allow you to make relatively inexpensive international calls from any public telephone. Making calls from hotels can turn out to be quite expensive.

7 Cell Phones
Cubacel is a cell phone service provider and has offices in most major cities and tourist centers. If you arrive in Cuba with your personal cell phone Cubacel can activate it, but it is extremely expensive.

8 Phone Codes
Local area codes may have 1 to 3 digits; the number of digits of local numbers varies. To call outside Cuba, dial 119, followed by the country code. To call Cuba from abroad, dial the international access number (00 in the UK, 011 in the US and Canada), then 53 and the local number.

9 Mail
Mail is dreadfully slow. Every town has a post office and most tourist hotels also sell stamps or prepaid postcards. All mail is read by censors. If sending anything important or valuable it is best to use DHL, which has offices in all major cities.

10 Laptops and Internet
All laptops must be declared when entering Cuba. You can log onto the Internet in many hotels and a few cyber cafés. However, the cost can vary widely. Access to the Internet for Cubans is limited to a privileged few.

Left **Medical sign** Center **A Cuban ambulance** Right **A local brand of mineral water**

🔟 Security and Health

1 Emergencies
The following numbers can be used in most places: 116 for police, 115 for fire services, and 114 for an ambulance. However, the police are not usually very responsive to reports of crimes against tourists and reporting theft can result in a lengthy bureaucratic procedure. In case of trouble, it is wise to contact your embassy or consulate. Asistur exists to assist tourists in distress and has offices in most tourist centers.

2 Health Services
Cuba's healthcare system is excellent and free of charge to Cubans. Foreign visitors are usually treated in international clinics. Payment is made in convertible pesos or by credit card, but fees are relatively inexpensive. Most tourist hotels have a doctor or nurse on call.

3 Pharmacies
Pharmaceuticals are in short supply, except in *farmacias internacionales* found in major cities and resorts. It is advisable to bring your own supply of medicines, as well as sunscreens and insect repellents.

4 Personal Safety
Violent crime against foreigners is rare, but in tourist areas and run-down sections of Havana, there is a risk of pick-pocketing and bag-snatching. Avoid dark and lonely spots, do not carry large amounts of cash, or flaunt expensive items. Theft from hotel rooms is a common occurrence, keep your possessions locked in your bag and your valuables in a safe.

5 Jineteros
Most visitors experience some level of harassment from individuals offering a range of services, but usually only in well-trodden tourist areas. *Jineteros* (male hustlers) will attempt to sell you fake cigars as the real thing; *jiniteras* are female prostitutes. The best way to deal with such situations is to give them the cold shoulder.

6 Police
Every town and village has its local police station but few officers speak English. If you are a victim of theft or are involved in an auto accident, contact your embassy, which should be able to help you.

7 Hitchhiking
Cubans hitchhike from necessity due to the poor public transportation system, although officials discourage foreigners from hitchhiking. Foreign embassies in Cuba report increasing robberies of foreigners by hitchhikers.

8 Women Travelers
Foreign women can receive a fair amount of unwanted attention from Cuban men, but this, for the most part, takes the form of harmless verbal intrusions. The most effective response to them is a stony glare or cold indifference.

9 Water
Do not drink the tap water. Some people prefer not to even brush their teeth with tap water. You should also make sure that ice cubes are made from purified water. Bottled water can be bought cheap and is widely available.

10 Food Hygiene
The best way to avoid an upset stomach is to steer clear of certain foods, notably lobster and fish dishes. Also stay clear of meats or dairy products that have been allowed to stand too long on a buffet counter or in the sun. Food from street stalls should be avoided.

Emergency

Asistur
• Paseo de Martí, Havana, (7) 866 4499
• 1ra Av. & 7, Varadero, (45) 66 7277 • Calle 4 & 7, Santiago de Cuba, (22) 68 6128
• www.asistur.cu

Police Stations
• Calle Picota, Havana, (7) 867 0496

Left **Spanish embassy in Havana** Center **Traffic police** Right **Cuban women greeting each other**

🔟 Practicalities

1 Consulates
Spain, Canada, and the UK have embassies in Havana with consular services. The US does not have a full embassy, but the US Interests Section provides assistance to travelers.

2 Legal Assistance
Contact your embassy or consulate for help immediately if you are arrested. The Consultoría Jurídica Internacional provides legal help and has branches in the major cities. ✆ *Consultoría Jurídica Internacional: Calle 16 #314, Miramar, Havana; (7) 204 2490*

3 Traffic Police
In the event of a car accident, call the traffic police *(tránsito)* and your car rental company. It is also wise to contact your embassy immediately. Do not allow any vehicles involved in the accident to be moved before the police arrive.

4 Bureaucracy
Bureaucracy pervades every aspect of Cuban life. Most services oriented to tourism function fluidly, although unbending regulations can make dealing with businesses and government institutions a frustrating experience.

5 Machismo
Despite advances in women's rights, *machismo* is ingrained in Cuba's male culture. This is mostly limited to flirtatious behavior to women but can also include expressions of bravado and even aggression intended to demonstrate male pride.

6 Homosexuality
Cuba's Communist government has a history of repressing homosexuality. However, in recent years, the government has been more lenient, and has even become supportive. Unfortunately, police harassment of homosexuals still occurs.

7 Dress Code
Cubans generally dress informally but are usually smartly turned out. Top restaurants require trousers as opposed to jeans or shorts for men. A collared shirt is a good idea for meetings.

8 Photography
It is common courtesy to ask permission before taking pictures of individuals. Photographs of police or military figures should not be taken without permission. Photographing industrial complexes, airports, ports, and military sites is strictly prohibited.

9 Racial Issues
Cuba enjoys harmonious relations between races. Mixed race marriages are common. However, racism has not been eradicated and black youths are the most likely targets.

10 Forms Of Greeting
Civility is important to Cubans, who greet everyone in a room when entering. Women embrace and kiss each other's cheeks, while men shake hands. Common greetings are *buen día* (good morning), *buenas tardes* (good afternoon), and *buenas noches* (good evening).

Embassies and Consulates

US
Calzada & L, Havana
• *(7) 833 3551*
Canada
Calle 30 #518, Havana
• *(7) 204 2516*
UK
Calle 34 #702, Havana
• *(7) 204 1771*
Spain
Cárcel and Zulueta
• *(7) 868 6868*

Major Public Holidays

• *1 Jan – Liberation Day*

• *2 Jan – Victory Day*

• *26 Jul – National Revolution Day*

• *10 Oct – Independence Day*

• *25 Dec – Christmas Day*

Left **Keeping out of the sun** Center **A common road hazard** Right **Swimming in the ocean**

🔟 Things to Avoid

1 Dehydration
It is easy to become dehydrated in Cuba's warm climate, where sweat often evaporates immediately. Drink plenty of bottled water and watch out for headaches, exhaustion, and muscle cramps, signs that you may be suffering from dehydration or heatstroke.

2 Sunstroke
Do not underestimate the power of the tropical sun. Sunburn and sunstroke are the most common health problems tourists encounter when visiting Cuba. Avoid the hottest part of the day, between noon and 3pm, and use a strong sunscreen, even when the weather is cloudy.

3 Traffic Accidents
Driving in Cuba can be dangerous due to the many road obstacles, as well as the lack of street lighting. Accidents involving injuries and deaths are considered a crime, and the guilty driver can be imprisoned.

4 Parking and Speeding Tickets
The traffic police are highly efficient and extremely zealous. Fines for speeding are deducted from the cash deposit of your car rental. Traffic police cannot levy fines on the spot, although unscrupulous policemen may try to do so. Keep to speed limits at all times.

5 Road Hazards
Cuba's roads have many surprises. In cities, cyclists and giant potholes are common threats. In the countryside, livestock often wander into the road. Freeways are especially hazardous due to the presence of pedestrians, ox-drawn carts, cyclists, and broken-down cars. Be prepared for animals and other obstacles moving into your path.

6 Driving At Night
Most Cuban roads are unlit, and lighting in cities is extremely poor. Many vehicles in Cuba do not have functioning lights. Avoid driving at night if possible.

7 Dangerous Rips and Undertows
Cuba's warm oceans tempt bathers to cool off and splash in the waves. However, many beaches are extremely dangerous due to hidden undertows that can drag swimmers out to sea. Beware of beaches with high surf.

8 Scams
Many Cubans are adept at scamming tourists. Scams range from *jiniteros* (hustlers) trying to sell fake cigars *(see p121)* and car rental agencies charging for unused gasoline, to taxi drivers overcharging tourists. Try to be alert to this as far as possible. Request an itemized bill at restaurants and hotels, and make sure that you count your change.

9 Prostitutes
Although prostitution is illegal in Cuba, many young women make a living as *jiniteras*, offering sexual favors for money. Robbery is frequent in these situations, and tourists have even been murdered. Countless other Cubans (male and female) seek relationships with foreigners. Strict regulations govern such sexual relations. *Casas particulares* will accept unmarried couples *(see p127)*. Tourists are rarely punished, but consequences for Cuban partners (and owners of *casas particulares*) can be dire.

10 Political Discourse
The Cuban government is highly sensitive to criticism of the Cuban system. Secret police and informers are ubiquitous. Thus, Cubans are extremely wary about discussing politics with people they do not know or trust. Avoid drawing people into conversations about politics, except in private, and foreigners should avoid making critical statements in public. Any tourists who meet with dissidents or visit "independent libraries" are also likely to face problems with the Cuban authorities.

Left **Street food stall** Right **A metrobus**

TOP 10 Budget Tips

Visit Off-Season
You can save a good deal both through booking package deals and as an independent traveler by visiting during the low season between June and November. The lowest rates are available September through mid-November during the peak of the hurricane season, but such storms are rare and this should not deter you.

Stay with Cuban Families
Overnight stays at *casas particulares (see p127)* are much cheaper than hotels and offer the opportunity of getting to know Cubans. Breakfast and sometimes dinner are served for an extra (but extremely reasonable) charge.

Street Food
Cheap food on sale at street stands presents a health risk, and the choices are extremely limited. A pizza or a plate of chicken with rice and beans will cost about five *pesos*. If you eat at a stall, make sure your food is freshly cooked. Avoid raw salads and fruits, as well as meat or fish dishes that have been left out in the sun.

Haggling
Bargaining is acceptable in souvenir markets. If you are persistent and polite, you may succeed in knocking down the price by one third or more. However, most souvenirs in Cuba are reasonably priced. Taxi drivers will negotiate a fare as they prefer not to use their meters; but find out what the metered fare should be in advance to avoid being taken advantage of.

Avoid Tourist Stores
Shops in hotels are often overpriced but there are few alternatives as all stores are state-owned. Souvenirs and art are cheaper if bought from the artists themselves or at craft markets that are set up at some of the beach resorts.

Public Transport
If you don't mind a little discomfort and unpredictability, traveling like a Cuban can save money. *Guaguas, camiones* and metrobuses *(see p118)* are a fraction of the cost of tourist buses and taxis and are a great way of meeting the locals. However, state officials try to dissuade foreigners from using public transport intended for Cubans.

Share a Guide
Guides normally charge a fixed fee, irrespective of the number of people in a group, so you can cut the cost of a guided tour by hiring a driver/guide for a day and sharing with other visitors. Taxis can also normally be shared between four people during trips.

Buy a Phone Card
Making calls from hotel rooms can be very expensive. The best and most economical solution is to buy a phone card *(see p120)*, which can be used in public phones, at some hotels, and in private phones, such as those at *casas particulares (see p127)*.

All-Inclusives
The all-inclusive hotels at beach resorts are immensely popular and can offer big savings over other hotels, as all food, beverages, and entertainment is included in your stay. Another benefit is that you can book all-inclusive package deals that include a reduced airfare. The downside is that you may be tempted not to leave the confines of the hotel.

Bring a Few Essentials from Home
Cuba's state-run stores impose huge price increases on all goods that are imported. Even local items produced in Cuba itself, such as suntan lotions and soaps, are expensive. You can save a considerable amount of money by bringing all toiletries and other essentials with you.

Left **A typical buffet** Center **A convenience store** Right **Produce at a** *mercado agropecuario*

🔟 Eating and Drinking Tips

1 Convenience Stores

The lack of restaurants and convenience stores between towns are the major drawbacks of visiting Cuba. When setting out on journeys, stock up on snacks at Tiendas Panamericanas, the state-run chain of convenience stores. You can also buy imported and packaged food items to supplement the inadequacies of hotel dining.

2 Fresh Fruit and Vegetables

Many hotels face a shortage of fresh fruits and vegetables. However, every town and village has at least one *mercado agropecuario* (farmer's market), where produce can be purchased for *pesos*. Visitors staying in *casas particulares (see p127)* may find this especially useful.

3 Breakfasts

A number of hotels serve typically simple breakfast buffets with cut meats, baked goods, and fruit (often thawed). All-inclusive hotels fare a little better. Other than hotels, few restaurants offer breakfast *(desayuno)* except in Havana, where French-run bakeries are a bargain.

4 Buffets

Many tourist hotels rely on smorgasbord buffets, called *mesa sueca* (Swiss table) where you will find a variety of dishes ranging from pastas and salads to roast suckling pig. Although the standards vary greatly, the pricier hotels are usually up to international standards.

5 Fried Food

Typical Cuban *criollo* cuisine is often deep-fried and heavy with oil. Even vegetables such as green beans often arrive at your table doused in oil. In order to avoid all the grease ask specifically for grilled meat or fish, known as *a la parrilla* or *a la plancha*.

6 Bills and Tipping

A 10 per cent service charge is often added to your bill, but no government tax is levied. It is unlikely that your waiter or waitress will end up with any of the service fee, so you should also leave a 10 per cent tip if you think the service merits it, although this is often not the case.

7 Alcoholic Drinks

Cuba excels in making refreshing lager-style beers, such as Cristal or Bucanero, and tasty rums with Havana Club being considered the best option *(see p57)*. Prices range from inexpensive in local bars to very expensive in deluxe hotels. Avoid imported beverages, which are also expensive. Wine is mostly imported from Spain or South America and is relatively expensive – and often stored in poor conditions.

8 Bars

Surprisingly, Cuba has few satisfying bars. Many of the pre-revolutionary bars still exist in their original format, but they mostly serve only tourists. Most of the other bars are much decayed and have a limited range of beers and rums. Hotel bars offer a level of sophistication, but are equally pricey and few Cubans can afford them.

9 Paladares

These are home-run restaurants that offer simple yet filling meals at reasonable prices. As the state restricts what can be sold here, lobster, shrimp, and beef dishes are usually not allowed. *Paladares* are banned entirely at beach resorts. If an individual on the street guides you to a *paladar* he or she will expect a commission from the owner who will add the fee to your bill.

10 Buy a Bottle

If you go out with a group in the evenings, it is customary to share a bottle of rum that comes with a bucket of ice, and you can order soft drinks as mixers. It is considerably cheaper compared to ordering individual drinks.

Left **Cycling** Center **Sportfishing boat** Right **A working steam train**

TOP 10 Tours and Special Interests

1 Tours of Habana Vieja

Although visitors can easily explore Old Havana independently on foot, anyone wishing for an in-depth profile should take a guided tour offered by Agencia San Cristóbal. An English-speaking guide will take you through the rich history associated with each sight. Decline the services of individuals presenting themselves on the streets as guides.

2 Excursions to Cayo Largo

Cubanacán and HavanaTur offer one- and two-day excursions from Havana and Varadero to the gorgeous beaches of Cayo Largo. Tour desks in most tourist hotels offer packages, which include airfare, accommodations, and airport transfers. ⊗ *Cubanacán: Calle 23 #156, Havana; (7) 833 4090; www.cubanacan.cu* • *Havanatur: Paseo & 25; (7) 830 8227; www.havanatur.cu*

3 Diving

There are superb diving sites around Cuba, which can provide exciting glimpses of underwater life throughout the year. Most beach resorts have scuba diving centers and Avalon Dive Center offers some fascinating dives. ⊗ *Avalon Dive Center: (33) 498 104; www.avalons.net*

4 Birding

For both amateurs and seasoned birders to appreciate the wealth of Cuba's birdlife, dedicated bird-watching tours can be arranged through EcoTur, Quest Nature Tours, and with guides from national parks. ⊗ *EcoTur: (7) 641 0306* • *Quest Nature Tours: (416) 633 5666; www.quest naturetours.com*

5 Cycling

Riding a bike is a rewarding way to get off the beaten track and experience rural life. Club Nacional de Cicloturismo offers organized group bicycle tours. Independ-ent cyclists can either bring along their own bikes or rent them.

6 Sportfishing

Marina Hemingway in Havana and most other marinas offer sportfishing charters. All such trips are operated by the state-run Marlin Náuticas & Marinas. Typical rates are CUC\$275 for a half-day and CUC\$375 for a full day. ⊗ *Marlin Náuticas & Marinas: (7) 273 1867*

7 The Revolutionaries

Anyone interested in revolutionary history cannot miss the venues associated with the Cuban Revolution, including sites in Havana, Santa Clara, Santiago de Cuba, and the Sierra Maestra (see p32).

8 Jewish Heritage Tours

Pre-revolution Havana had a large Jewish population in southern Habana Vieja (see p8), and many Jewish sites have been restored. Start at Casa de la Comunidad Hebrea de Cuba. ⊗ *Comunidad Hebrea de Cuba: Calle I #241, Havana, (7) 832 8953*

9 Hemingway Trail

Ernest Hemingway (see p61) wrote a large number of his most influential books during his 20 years on the island and frequented many venues around the capital. Visitors like to pursue the "Hemingway Trail" that traces the sites in Havana and along the north coast of Cuba. Paradiso offers guided tours of such sites around Havana. ⊗ *Paradiso: Calle 19 #560, Havana, (7) 832 6928; http:// paradisonline.com*

10 Steam Train Enthusiasts

Although the first railway on the island pre-dated the establishment of trains on the Spanish mainland, Cuba's remarkable collection of working steam trains is rapidly dwindling (see p61). Museums of trenes de vapores (steam trains) still exist in Havana, Maltiempo, and Rafael Freyre. Several other locations offer rides too.

Left **The interior of a *casa particular*** Center **Parking** Right **Licensed room rental sticker**

Accommodation Tips

1 Pick Your Location

In general, beachfront hotels will cost more than those off the beach, and a room with a sea view will be costlier still. Being miles from sites of interest, most beach hotels are all-inclusives, and guests are not expected to stray far except on excursions. In Havana and historic cities, choose a hotel close to the colonial core for ease of exploring.

2 Seasonal Demand

Prior booking is essential during the peak season around Christmas and New Year and is also recommended from January to March. Locally, hotels also fill up for festivals such as the *Carnaval (see p52)* in Santiago de Cuba and the *parrandas (see p88)* in Remedios.

3 Casas Particulares

Renting rooms in private homes *(see p17)* is rewarding for visitors who want to experience everyday Cuban family life. Conditions at *casas particulares* are fairly simple, but the cost is less than hotels and the experience is priceless. Home-cooked meals are often available for a little extra. Most *casas particulares* will accept unmarried couples. Licensed room rentals are identified by an official sticker resembling an inverted anchor.

4 Making Reservations

Accommodation should be booked well in advance through a travel agency specializing in Cuba in your home country. Reservations made directly with Cuban hotels are not always honored but owners of *casas particulares* are usually reliable.

5 Arriving Without Reservations

It is possible to travel everywhere off season without advance booking, but the high season is more problematic. If a *casa particular* is full, the owner will call around town on your behalf to find you a vacant room.

6 Tipping

Tipping is customary for hotel staff although it is at your own discretion. Tip porters CUC$1 per bag carried to your room. If you leave CUC$1 daily in your room you are less likely to suffer theft of personal items by housekeepers.

7 All-Inclusives

Quality varies markedly at all-inclusive hotels, but in general you get what you pay for. The buffet may get monotonous and alcohol is limited to national brands of rum and beer with watered-down wine for dinner. In theory, everything is included in your room rate, but check

in advance to see what extra charges may apply. In general, those managed by foreign companies are of higher standard than the locally-managed all-inclusives.

8 Air Conditioning

Almost every hotel and *casa particular* has air conditioning. Large tourist hotels have a back-up generator, but smaller hotels often suffer blackouts. Some hotels also have ceiling fans, and *casa particular* owners will usually provide a standing fan if you request one.

9 Visitors with Disabilities

Very few hotels have facilities for the disabled, although recently built or renovated hotels usually have at least one room that is fitted with facilities for disabled travelers. Cuban society, on the whole, is very caring toward disabled people and hotel managers will try to make their stay as comfortable as possible.

10 Parking

Most large tourist hotels have adequate parking facilities for rental cars. However, smaller inner-city hotels and *casas particulares* rarely do. In such cases, inquire about a secure parking lot that is well-guarded to ensure the safety of your vehicle.

Make sure to keep your valuables safe as theft from hotel rooms can occur.

Streetsmart

Left **Hostal Valencia** Center **Hotel Arenas Doradas** Right **Hotel Colón**

Budget Hotels

Hostal Valencia, Habana Vieja

In the style of a Spanish *bodega*, this small historic hotel lies in the heart of Habana Vieja. The rooms are simple and individual with cool marble floors. The restaurant is known for its paella. ◈ *Map X1 • Calle Oficios 53 • (7) 867 1037 • www.habaguanex. com • $$$*

Hotel Caribbean, Habana Vieja

This inexpensive hotel is conveniently located on Paseo de Martí in Centro Habana. The clean air-conditioned rooms are in lively color schemes and have satellite TV, safes, and phones. The ground-floor café opens onto the loud thoroughfare. ◈ *Map W1 • Paseo de Martí 164 • (7) 860 8241 • www. islazul.cu • $$*

Hotel Arenas Doradas, Varadero

An all-inclusive with a non-inclusive option, this beachfront resort has a pool and a choice of restaurants. It is perhaps the best value option in Varadero for visitors who would like to explore around town. ◈ *Map F2 • Autopista Sur, km 17 • (45) 66 8150 • reserve@ arena.gca.tur.cu • $$$*

Villa Los Caneyes, Santa Clara

Popular with tour groups, this hotel on the outskirts of town has comfortable,

octagonal, thatched cabins with air conditioning and satellite TV. The elegant restaurant has buffet and à la carte meals. A poolside fashion show is held nightly. ◈ *Map H3 • Av. de los Eucaliptos • (42) 21 8140 • www.hotelescubanacan. com • $$$*

Hotel Mascotte, Remedios

This renovated historic hotel is situated just off the main plaza. All 10 rooms have modern bathrooms, and the restaurant is one of the nicest in town. ◈ *Map J2 • Calle Máximo Gómez 114 • (42) 39 5144 • www.hoteles cubanacan.com • $$*

La Casona de Morón, Morón

The hotel, a colonial mansion a stone's throw from the train station, is within walking distance of the town center. A marble stairway leads to the seven large rooms with modern bathrooms, safes, and ceiling fans. The pool is a bonus, and the lawn is a venue for an earth-shattering disco Thursday to Sunday nights. ◈ *Map K2 • Calle Cristóbal Colón 41 • (33) 50 2236 • $*

Hotel Colón, Camagüey

A delightfully historic hotel, Hotel Colón has been restored and upgraded. One room is equipped for disabled

travelers. A gleaming mahogany bar is a great place for cocktails, whilst the restaurant is considered the city's most elegant. ◈ *Map L3 • Av. República 472 • (32) 28 3368 • www.islazul.cu • $$*

Hotel Niquero, Niquero

A surprisingly modern hotel in this remote, dilapidated town near Parque Desambarco del Granma *(see p47)*. The rooftop bar serves good cocktails. ◈ *Map M5 • Calle Martí & Céspedes • (23) 59 2367 • $*

Hotel Libertad, Santiago de Cuba

Offering good value for money, this budget option overlooks Parque Marte and is situated close to sites of interest. Rooms are small but offer essential amenities. The hotel has an Internet café, a pleasant restaurant, and a disco. ◈ *Map P6 • Calle Aguilera 658 • (22) 62 8360 • www. islazul.cu • $$*

Brisas Sierra Mar, Chivirico

This popular, bargain-priced all-inclusive hotel is set on a headland overlooking a beach. Excursions include one to Santiago de Cuba, which is an hour's drive away. ◈ *Map N6 • Carretera de Chivirico, km 60 • (22) 32 9110 • www.hoteles cubanacan.com • ventas@ smar.scu.tur.cu • $$$*

Price Categories

For a standard double room per night with breakfast (if included), taxes, and extra charges.	**$** under CUC$30
	$$ CUC$30–50
	$$$ CUC$50–100
	$$$$ CUC$100–150
	$$$$$ over CUC$150

Casa de Juan Sánchez, Cienfuegos

🔟 Private Room Rentals

1 Casa de Jorge Coalla, Havana

A gracious family hosts visitors in this one-room *casa particular* superbly located in Vedado, close to key sites and restaurants. The spacious, air-conditioned room is well-equipped and the bathroom has lots of hot water. 🗺 *Map S1 • Calle I #456, Vedado • (7) 832 9032 • www.havanaroomrental. com • jorgepotts@yahoo. co.uk • $*

2 Casa de Elena Sánchez, Havana

This 1950s two-story home can be rented entirely. It has eclectic furnishings in the lounge and two bedrooms. A garden and secure parking are an added bonus. It is, however, a long distance from Habana Vieja. 🗺 *Calle 34 #714, Miramar • (7) 202 8969 • gerardo@enet.cu*

3 Casa de Juan Sánchez, Cienfuegos

Dramatic Modernist architecture is the appeal of this 1950s home in the Punta Gorda district. The single bedroom is cross-ventilated and has a well-kept bathroom. 🗺 *Map G3 • Av. 8 #3703 • (43) 51 7986 • $*

4 Casa de Jorge Rivero, Remedios

This well-maintained 1950s home very close to the main square has two bedrooms. The one upstairs has a lounge, large bathroom, and an independent entrance. The other has a smaller bathroom. 🗺 *Map J2 • Calle Brigadier González 29 • (42) 39 6538 • $*

5 Casa Colonial Muñoz, Trinidad

A spacious 18th-century home full of antiques. The knowledgeable and friendly Muñoz family speaks English and can assist travelers. Each of the two bedrooms have bathrooms ensuite. Delicious dinners are served. 🗺 *Map H4 • Calle Martí 401 • (41) 99 3673 • http://casa.trinidadphoto. com • trinidadjulio@yahoo. com • $$*

6 Casa de Carlos Sotolongo, Trinidad

Facing the Plaza Mayor, this superbly situated colonial home combines colonial-era antiques with contemporary art. The two gracious rooms with en suite bathrooms feature terracotta floors and wrought-iron beds. 🗺 *Map H4 • Calle Rúben Martínez Villena 33 • (41) 99 4169 • $$*

7 Villa Liba, Holguín

A short walk from both downtown and the Loma de Cruz, this 1950s house is owned by a well-educated, friendly couple. The two spacious guest rooms are air-conditioned and have period furnishings. Filling meals are served on the patio. It has secure parking. 🗺 *Map N4 • Calle Maceo 46 • (24) 42 3823 • $*

8 Villa Formell, Holguín

Just a couple of blocks from the Parque Calixto García, this large house is run by the cousin of Juan Formell, founder of a famous Cuban salsa group. The comfortable guest room has its own bathroom, and there's a leafy shared patio. 🗺 *Map N4 • Calle Morales Lemus 189 • (24) 42 2547 • $*

9 Casa de Adrián y Tonia, Manzanillo

This friendly home is only steps away from Monumento Celia Sánchez, the town's main site. The independent upstairs apartment is air conditioned and also has fans, plus a modern bathroom, kitchen and its own roof terrace. Guests can use the host's TV lounge. 🗺 *Map M5 • Calle Mártires de Viet Nam 49 • (23) 57 3028 • sbeltran@ golfo.grm.sld.cu • $*

10 Casa Colonial Maruchi, Santiago de Cuba

At one of the city's most professionally run *casas particulares* two guest rooms feature colonial-period furniture and share a bathroom. A peacock roams the delightful central patio. 🗺 *Map P6 • Calle Hartman (San Félix) 357 • (22) 62 0767 • $*

Left **Hotel Conde de Villanueva** Center **Hostal Los Frailes** Right **Hotel NH Parque Central**

🔟 Havana Hotels

1 Hotel Raquel
A stylish historic hotel with tremendous Art Nouveau decor and an excellent location just one block from Plaza Vieja. Facilities include a gym and solarium. ✪ *Map X2 • Amargura & San Ignacio, Habana Vieja • (7) 860 8280 • www. habaguanex.com • $$$$*

2 Hostal Los Frailes
Themed as a monastery with staff that dress as monks, this hotel has cozy rooms with wrought-iron furnishings surrounding a patio. There is no restaurant, but nearby Plaza Vieja has several options. ✪ *Map X2 • Calle Brasil between Oficios & Mercaderes, Habana Vieja • (7) 862 9383 • www. habaguanex.com • $$$*

3 Hotel Conde de Villanueva
In the heart of Habana Vieja, the former mansion of the Count of Villanueva offers nine intimate rooms facing an airy courtyard. A cigar lounge draws serious smokers. ✪ *Map X1 • Calle Mercaderes 202, Habana Vieja • (7) 862 9293 • www.habaguanex.com • $$$$*

4 Hotel Florida
A magnificent colonial conversion and a haven of peace on Habana Vieja's busiest street, this sumptuous hotel is centered on a courtyard.

It has spacious rooms furnished in colonial style with wrought-iron beds. ✪ *Map X1 • Calle Obispo 252, Habana Vieja • (7) 862 4127 • www.habaguanex. com • $$$$*

5 Hotel NH Parque Central
This luxury option overlooks Havana's liveliest square with elegant rooms that feature reproduction antiques and Internet connections. It has a classy lobby bar, two fine restaurants, boutiques, and a rooftop swimming pool. Popular with business travelers. ✪ *Map W1 • Calle Neptuno between Prado & Zulueta • (7) 860 6627 • www. nh-hotels.cu • $$$$$*

6 Hotel Saratoga
The most sophisticated hotel in town, this stylish restoration of a historic hotel merges colonial and ultra-contemporary features. Rooms have DVD players, Internet connections, and posh furnishings. A fabulous restaurant, chic bar, and rooftop pool complete the picture. ✪ *Map W1 • Paseo de Martí 603, Habana Vieja • (7) 868 1000 • www.hotel-saratoga.com • $$$$$*

7 Hotel Victoria
A solid bargain, this small and unpretentious hotel has a wood-paneled restaurant and is close to many of the areas

restaurants and nightclubs. Rooms are small but adequate. ✪ *Map U1 • Calle 19 #101, Vedado • (7) 833 3510 • www. hotelvictoriacuba.com • $$$*

8 Hotel Nacional
Built in the 1930s, this gracious grand-dame is considered Havana's top hotel. It has four restaurants and six bars, including a lovely garden terrace bar and the Cabaret Parisien (see p71). Many rooms are dowdy so take an executive floor room. ✪ *Map U1 • Calle O & 21, Vedado • (7) 836 3564 • www.hotelnacionaldecuba. com • $$$$$*

9 Hotel Habana Libre Tryp
The key attractions of this 1950s high-rise in the heart of Vedado include a bank, a leading nightclub, a business center, tour desks, and a pool. Rooms have modern amenities but cleanliness is not guaranteed. ✪ *Map U1 • Calle L & 23, Vedado • (7) 838 4011 • www. gran-caribe.com • $$$$*

10 Occidental Miramar
This large, upscale hotel has a plethora of facilities and suave contemporary styling that extends to the guest rooms. The three restaurants are par excellence. ✪ *5ta Av. & 72, Miramar • (7) 204 3584 • www.occidental-hoteles. com • $$$$$*

Price Categories

For a standard double room per night with breakfast (if included), taxes, and extra charges.

$	under CUC30
$$	CUC30–50
$$$	CUC50–100
$$$$	CUC100–150
$$$$$	over CUC150

Interior of Hotel Unión, Cienfuegos

🔟 Town Center Hotels

1 Hotel Vuelta Abajo, Pinar del Río

This small, colonial-era hotel with spacious, simply-furnished rooms has a no-frills restaurant and bar, plus Internet service. Rooms with a balcony cost a little more. Its downtown location is handy, but street noise can be a nuisance. ◈ *Map B3 • Calle Martí 103 • (48) 75 9381 • $$*

2 Hotel La Unión, Cienfuegos

Restored to its original 19th-century glory, Hotel Unión is the town's best. Its comfortable rooms surround a pretty courtyard with a fountain. ◈ *Map G3 • Calle 31 & Av. 54 • (43) 55 1020 • www. hotelescubanacan.com • $$$*

3 Hostal del Rijo, Sancti Spíritus

A delightful colonial conversion on a charming plaza, this bargain-priced option has spacious rooms with modern marble bathrooms. Breakfast is provided, but there is no restaurant. ◈ *Map J3 • Calle Honorato del Castillo 12 • (41) 32 8588 • www.hoteles cubanacan.com • $$*

4 Iberostar Gran Hotel Trinidad, Trinidad

This deluxe, inner-city hotel opened in 2006. A gleaming marble staircase leads to 45 luxurious rooms and a restaurant that is one of the finest outside Havana. A billiards room and cigar lounge are pluses. ◈ *Map H4 • Calle Martí 262 • (41) 99 6070 • www.iberostar.com • $$$$*

5 Gran Hotel, Camagüey

A classic hotel that has been restored to its former grandeur. The top-floor restaurant has good views and serves excellent buffets. Nicely furnished, air-conditioned rooms offer safes, satellite TVs, and modern bathrooms. ◈ *Map L3 • Calle Maceo 67 • (32) 29 2093 • www.islazul.cu • $$*

6 Hotel Royalton, Bayamo

Built in the 1940s, this hotel is centrally located on the main square. The air-conditioned rooms, though not fancy, are comfortable, with TVs and clean bathrooms. ◈ *Map N5 • Calle Maceo 53 • (23) 42 2268 • www. islazul.cu• $$*

7 Hostal San Basilio, Santiago de Cuba

An intimate and friendly hotel close to Parque Céspedes, this restored colonial mansion has a restaurant and 24-hour bar. The clean rooms are simple, with phones, safes, and TVs. ◈ *Map P6 • Calle San Basilio 403 • (22) 65 1702 • www. hotelescubanacan.com • $$*

8 Hotel Casagranda, Santiago de Cuba

This magnificent colonial-era hotel on the main square offers refurbished rooms with reproduction antique furniture and modern accoutrements. The restaurant offers gourmet cuisine, and the rooftop terrace bar offers great views and a lively social scene. ◈ *Map P6 • Calle Heredia 201 • (22) 68 6600 • www.gran-caribe. com • $$$$*

9 Hostal La Habanera, Baracoa

The simply furnished rooms in this small, colonial hotel come with satellite TVs, fridges, and modern bathrooms. Massages are offered and there's a pleasant restaurant. Other features include Internet service as well as a clinic. ◈ *Map R5 • Calle Maceo 126 • (21) 64 5273 • www.islazul.cu • $$*

10 Hotel El Castillo, Baracoa

The place to stay for postcard views of Baracoa and the unique El Yunque mountain *(see p27)*, the rooms in this former fortress are comfortable and well-appointed with colonial furnishings. The town's best restaurant is here too. A pool and tour desk are bonuses. ◈ *Map R5 • Loma de Paraíso • (21) 64 5165 • www.gaviota-grupo. com • $$$*

Left **Hotel & Villa Turística Soroa** Center **Hotel Las Jazmines** Right **Villa Mirador de Mayabe**

™10 Rural Hotels

1 Hotel & Villa Turística Soroa, Soroa

Surrounded by forested hills, this bucolic option has a lovely natural setting centered on a swimming pool. Choose from comfy cabins or spacious self-catering villas with private pools. ✪ Map C2 • Carretera de Soroa, km 8 • (48) 52 3534 • www.hotelescubanacan. com • $$$

2 Hotel La Moka, Las Terrazas

Poised over Las Terrazas village and shrouded in woodland, this colonial-themed hotel focuses on ecotourism, with a lobby that is built around a tree. Rooms offer scenic forest views. ✪ Map C2 • Autopista Habana-Pinar del Río, km 51 • (48) 57 8600 • asistente@ commoka.get.tur.cu • $$$

3 Rancho San Vicente, Viñales

This refuge in a wooded valley features simple air-conditioned cabins, with porches and huge windows. A lovely restaurant adjoins the pool. ✪ Map B2 • Carretera a Puerto Esperanza, km 33 • (48) 79 6201 • www.hoteles cubanacan.com • $$$

4 Hotel Las Jazmines, Viñales

Housed in an original 1950s Neo-Colonial structure, this hotel has a spectacular hilltop setting that guarantees incredible views. Of the three room types, the most comfortable are in the modern annex. ✪ Map B2 • Carretera a Viñales, km 23 • (48) 79 6205 • www.hoteles cubanacan.co • $$$

5 Villa San José del Lago, Mayajigua

On the north coast road of Sancti Spíritus province, this peaceful complex features thermal swimming pools and a lake with rowboats and flamingos. Air-conditioned cabins are simple yet comfy. Popular with Cubans, it comes alive on weekends. ✪ Map J2 • Avenida Antonio Guiteras • (41) 54 6108 • www. islazul.cu • $$

6 Motel La Belén, El Pilar

This off-the-beaten-track hotel in Sierra del Chorillo, southeast of Camagüey city, appeals to nature lovers. The five spacious rooms have modern bathrooms and there is a cozy lounge plus swimming pool. The restaurant serves buffalo. ✪ Map L4 • Comunidad El Pilar • (32) 29 9208 • $

7 Villa Mirador de Mayabe, Mayabe

Perched atop a hill with spectacular valley views, this villa has a cliff-top swimming pool and thatched restaurant which are popular with tour groups and locals. The refitted cabins have air conditioning, satellite TVs, fridges, and telephones. ✪ Map N4 • Alturas de Mayabe, km 8 • (24) 42 2160 • www. islazul.cu • $$

8 Villa Pinares de Mayarí, Pinares de Mayarí

This mountain resort offers hiking, bird-watching, and mountain biking. It is set amid a pine forest and can only be reached via a daunting unpaved road. ✪ Map P5 • La Mensura • (24) 50 3308 • www.gaviota-grupo. com • $$

9 Villa Cayo Saetía, Cayo Saetía

On a forested island once utilized for hunting by Communist officials, this coastal cabin complex features pleasant furnishings. The rustic restaurant is adorned with animal heads. ✪ Map P4 • Cayo Saetía • (24) 519 6900 • www. gaviota-grupo.com • $$$

10 Hotel El Saltón, El Saltón

Focused on ecotourism, this riverside hotel is surrounded by forest. Rooms are simply furnished but have satellite TV. The restaurant overlooks a cascade. Guided hikes and bird-watching are available. ✪ Map N5 • Carretera Filé, Tercer Frente • (22) 56 6326 • www.hotelescubanacan. com • $$

Price Categories

For a standard double room per night with breakfast (if included), taxes, and extra charges.

$	under CUC$30
$$	CUC$30–50
$$$	CUC$50–100
$$$$	CUC$100–150
$$$$$	over CUC$150

Barceló Marina Palace Resort, Varadero

🔟 Beach Hotels

1 Hotel María La Gorda, María La Gorda
This isolated, end-of-the-road hotel specializes in diving and sportfishing. Choose simple modern rooms or bungalows, or rustic but comfy cabins. Cash only, and reservations are advisable. ◐ Map A4 • (48) 77 8131 • www.gaviota-grupo.com • $$$

2 Sol Cayo Largo, Cayo Largo
A classy all-inclusive resort on a spectacular stretch of white sand. Sol Cayo Largo has a pool and several restaurants. The rooms are painted in ice-cream pastels. ◐ Map F4 • Playa Lindamar • (45) 24 8260 • www.solmelia cuba.com • $$$$$

3 Mansión Xanadu, Varadero
In the former mansion of the DuPont family, this deluxe hotel has seven huge, marble-floored guest rooms, an excellent restaurant, and an atmospheric bar with live music. Guests get golf privileges. ◐ Map F2 • Autopista del Sur, km 8.5 • (45) 66 7388 • www.varaderogolfclub.com • $$$$$

4 Barceló Solymar Beach Resort, Varadero
A colorful all-inclusive hotel with contemporary furnishings, a huge pool, and plenty of facilities. Choose handsome hotel rooms or modern bungalows. The town is within walking distance. ◐ Map F2 • Av. Las Américas, km 3 • (45) 61 4499 • www.barcelo.com • $$$$$

5 Sandals Royal Hicacos Resort and Spa, Varadero
Near the far east end of the peninsula, this resplendent, all-suite all-inclusive resorts for couples only has some of the most romantic rooms in Varadero, all with king-size beds. There are five restaurants and impressive entertainment. ◐ Map F2 • Carretera de las Morlas, km 15 • (45) 66 8844 • www.sandals hicacos.com • $$$$$

6 Barceló Marina Palace Resort, Varadero
This deluxe all-inclusive resort has nautically themed decor. Rooms are equipped with state-of-the-art amenities, and the pool has a huge spiral waterslide. However, its location at the remote eastern tip of the peninsula is a long way from town. ◐ Map F2 • Punta Hicacos Final • (45) 66 9966 • www.barcelo.com • $$$$$

7 Meliá Cayo Santa María, Cayo Santa María
An elegant all-inclusive with a vast pool complex, a choice of gourmet restaurants, lively entertainment, and plenty of watersports. ◐ Map J1 • (42) 35 0200 • www.solmeliacuba.com • $$$$

8 Brisas Trinidad del Mar, Playa Ancón
Architecture at this modern, Neo-Classical style all-inclusive hotels integrates elements inspired by the colonial buildings of nearby Trinidad. Rooms have modern amenities. ◐ Map H4 • Peninsula Ancón • (41) 99 6500 • www.hotelescubanacan.com • $$$$

9 Meliá Cayo Coco
A chic all-inclusive that outshines other hotels on the island. This hotel caters to adults only and room options include two-story cabins overhanging a lagoon. It has three restaurants and a cigar lounge. ◐ Map K2 • Cayo Coco • (33) 30 1180 • www.solmeliacuba.com • $$$$$

10 Occidental Grand Playa Turquesa, Guardalavaca
This huge yet gracious all-inclusive is built around seven swimming pools connected by waterfalls. The facilities include five restaurants, six bars, and sports and entertainment for both adults and children. ◐ Map P4 • Playa Yuraguanal • (24) 43 3540 • www.occidental-hoteles.com • $$$$$

General Index

Acknowledgements

Author

Christopher P. Baker is an award-winning travel writer and photographer specializing in the Caribbean and Central America. His feature articles have appeared in more than 200 publications worldwide. His many books include the literary travelog *Mi Moto Fidel: Motorcycling Through Castro's Cuba*.

AT DORLING KINDERSLEY

Publisher Douglas Amrine

List Manager Christine Stroyan

Managing Art Editor Mabel Chan

Senior Editor Ros Walford

Project Designers Paul Jackson, Shahid Mahmood

Senior Cartographic Editor Casper Morris

Senior Cartographic Designer Suresh Kumar

Cartographer Zafar-ul-Islam Khan

DTP Operator Natasha Lu

Production Anna Wilson

Photographer Tony Souter

Additional Photography Ernesto Juan Castellanos, Claire Jones

Fact Checking Ernesto Juan Castellanos

Revisions Jude Ledger, Carly Madden, Nicola Malone, Sonal Modha

Picture Credits

t=top; tc=top center; tr=top right; cla=center left above; ca=center above; cra=center right above; cl=center left; c=center; cr=center right; clb=center left below; cb=center below; crb=center right below; bl=bottom left; bc=bottom center; br=bottom right.

The photographer, writers and publisher would like to thank the media staff at the following sights and organizations for their helpful cooperation:

4CORNERS IMAGES: SIME/ Schmid Reinhard 7cr.

ALAMY: Adam Picture Library 52bl; AEP 32bl; Rachael Bowes 6bl; Joep Clason 48bl; isafa Image Service s.r.o. 88b, 111tl; geophotos 26cla; JHQ 22-23c; LOOK Die Bildagentur der Fotografen GmbH/Sabine Lubenow 48tl; 49tr; Melba Photo Agency 78tl; John Norman 20-21c;

Pictures Colour Library 24-25c; Picture Contact/ Jochem Wijnands 56 tl; POPPERFOTO 31cl; Robert Harding Pictures Library Ltd/ Bruno Morandi 23cr; SAS 86cr; Alex Segre 85tl; 120tl; Tribaleye Images/J. Marshall 34c; Visions of America LLC/ Joe Sohm 46tl.

Courtesy of CERNUDA ARTE:40tl, 41tl.

CORBIS: Bettmann 30bl; Tibor Bognar 96tl; Hemis/ Geoges Antoni 14-15c; Kim Kulish 122tc; Milepost 92 ½/ Colin Garrett 80br; Donald Nausbaum 76-77; Jose Fuste Raga 1c; Robert Harding World Imagery/Ellen Rooney 104-5; Robert van der Hitst 34tc; Andre St George 34bl; Sygma/Sophie Bassouls 40tr.

GETTY IMAGES: Time & Life Pictures/Lee Lockwood 30t.

MASTERFILE: Alberto Biscaro 28-29, 62-63.

ANDREA PISTOLESI: 102tr.

REUTERS: Oswaldo Rivas 53bl.

LUCIO ROSSI: 7br, 15cr, 26-27c, 50tl, 50c, 50bl, 51bl, 84tl, 87bl, 102tl, 112tl, 117tr.

VISAGE MEDIA SERVICES: Peter Adams 49tr; Cesar Lucas Abreu 2tl,106c; Agnelo Cavalli 114-5; Grant Faint 60cl; Carl Mydans 35cl; Steve Winter 6cb.

WIKIMEDIA COMMONS: 40c.

WIKIPEDIA, The Free Encyclopedia: Friman: http:// en.wikipedia.org/wiki/ Wikipedia:Text_of_the_GNU_ Free_Documentation_ Licence: 81cl.

All other images © Dorling Kindersley.

For further information see:

www.dkimages.com

Special Editions of DK Travel Guides

Phrase Book

The Spanish spoken in Cuba is basically the same as the Castilian used in Spain with certain deviations. As in the Spanish-speaking countries in Central and Southern America, the "z" is pronounced like the "s," as is the "c" when it comes before "e" or "i." Among the grammatical variations, visitors should be aware that Cubans use *Ustedes* in place of *Vosotros*, to say "you" when referring to more than one person. It is notable that some Indian, African, and English words are commonly used in present-day Cuban Spanish. This basic phrase book includes useful common phrases and words, and particular attention has been paid to typically Cuban idioms in a list of Cuban Terms.

Emergencies

Help!	**¡socorro!**	sokorro
Stop!	**¡pare!**	pareh
Call a doctor	**Llamen un médico**	yamen oon medeeko
Call an ambulance	**Llamen a una ambulancia**	yamen a oona amboolans-ya
Police!	**¡policía!**	poleesee-a
I've been robbed	**Me robaron**	meh robaron

Communication Essentials

Yes	**sí**	see
No	**no**	no
Please	**por favor**	por fabor
Pardon me	**perdone**	pairdoneh
Excuse me	**disculpe**	deeskoolpeh
I'm sorry	**lo siento**	lo s-yento
Thanks	**gracias**	gras-yas
Hello!	**¡buenas!**	bwenas
Good day	**buenos días**	bwenos dee-as
Good afternoon	**buenas tardes**	bwenas tardes
Good evening	**buenas noches**	bwenas noches
night	**noche**	nocheh
morning	**mañana**	man-yana
tomorrow	**mañana**	man-yana
yesterday	**ayer**	a-yair
Here	**acá**	aka
How?	**¿cómo?**	komo
When?	**¿cuándo?**	kwando
Where?	**¿dónde?**	dondeh
Why?	**¿por qué?**	por keh
How are you?	**¿qué tal?**	keh tal
It's a pleasure!	**¡mucho gusto!**	moocho goosto
Goodbye	**hasta luego**	asta lwego

Useful Phrases

That's fine	**está bien/ocá**	esta b-yen/oka
Fine	**¡qué bien!**	keh b-yen
How long?	**¿Cuánto falta?**	kwanto falta
Do you speak a little English?	**¿Habla un poco de inglés?**	abla oon poko deh eengles
I don't understand	**No entiendo**	no ent-yendo
Could you speak more slowly?	**¿Puede hablar más despacio?**	pwedeh ablas mas despas-yo
I agree/OK	**de acuerdo/ocá**	deh akwairdo/oka

Certainly!	**¡Claro que sí!**	klaro keh see!
Let's go!	**¡Vámonos!**	bamonos

Useful Words

large	**grande**	grandeh
small	**pequeño**	peken-yo
hot	**caliente**	kal-yenteh
cold	**frío**	free-o
good	**bueno**	bweno
bad	**malo**	malo
so-so	**más o menos**	mas o menos
well/fine	**bien**	b-yen
open	**abierto**	ab-yairto
closed	**cerrado**	serrado
full	**lleno**	yeno
empty	**vacío**	basee-o
right	**derecha**	dairecha
left	**izquierda**	isk-yairda
straight	**recto**	rrekto
under	**debajo**	debaho
over	**arriba**	arreeba
quickly/early	**pronto/temprano**	pronto/temprano
late	**tarde**	tardeh
now	**ahora**	a-ora
soon	**ahorita**	a-oreeta
more	**más**	mas
less	**menos**	menos
little	**poco**	poko
sufficient	**suficiente**	soofees-yenteh
much	**mucho/muy**	moocho/mwee
too much	**demasiado**	demas-yado
in front of	**delante**	delanteh
behind	**detrás**	detras
first floor	**primer piso**	preemair peeso
ground floor	**planta baja**	planta baha
lift/elevator	**elevador**	elebador
bathroom/toilet	**servicios**	sairbees-yos
women	**mujeres**	moohaires
men	**hombres**	ombres
toilet paper	**papel sanitario**	papel saneetar-yo
camera	**cámara**	kamara
batteries	**baterías**	bataree-as
passport	**pasaporte**	pasaporteh
visa; tourist card	**visa; tarjeta turística**	beesa; tarheta tooreesteeka

Transport

Could you call a taxi for me?	**¿Me puede llamar un taxi?**	meh pwedeh yamar oon taksee?
airport	**aeropuerto**	a-airopwairto
train station	**estación de ferrocarriles**	estas-yon deh fairrokarreeles
bus station	**terminal de autobús**	tairmeenal deh owtoboos
When does it leave?	**¿A qué hora sale?**	a keh ora saleh?
customs	**aduana**	adwana
boarding pass	**tarjeta de embarque**	tarheta deh embarkeh
car hire	**alquiler de carros**	alkeelair deh karros
bicycle	**bicicleta**	beeseekleta
insurance	**seguro**	segooro
petrol/gas station	**estación de gasolina**	estas-yon deh gasoleena

Staying in a Hotel

single room/ double	**habitación sencilla/ doble**	abeetas-yon sensee-ya /dobleh
shower	**ducha**	doocha
bathtub	**bañera**	ban-yaira
balcony	**balcón, terraza**	balkon, tairrasa
warm water	**agua caliente**	agwa kal-yenteh
cold water	**agua fría**	agwa free-a
soap	**jabón**	habon
towel	**toalla**	to-a-ya
key	**llave**	yabeh

Eating Out

What is there to eat?	**¿Qué hay para comer?**	keh I para komair?
The bill please	**la cuenta por favor**	la kwenta por fabor
I would like some water	**Quisiera un poco de agua**	kees-yaira oon poko deh agwa
Have you got wine?	**¿Tienen vino?**	t-yenen beeno?
The beer is not cold enough	**La cerveza no está bien fría**	la sairbesa no esta b-yen free-a
breakfast	**desayuno**	desa-yoono
lunch	**almuerzo**	almwairso
dinner	**comida**	komeeda
raw/cooked	**crudo/cocido**	kroodo/koseedo
glass	**vaso**	baso
cutlery	**cubiertos**	koob-yairtos

Menu Decoder

aceite	asayteh	oil
agua mineral	agwa meenairal	mineral water
aguacate	agwakateh	avocado
ajo	aho	garlic
arroz	arros	rice
asado	asado	roasted
atún	atoon	tuna
azúcar	asookar	sugar
bacalao	bakala-o	cod
café	kafeh	coffee
camarones	kamarones	prawns
carne	karneh	meat
congrí	kongree	rice with beans and onions
cerveza	sairbesa	beer
dulce	doolseh	sweet, dessert
ensalada	ensalada	salad
fruta	froota	fruit
fruta bomba	froota bomba	papaya
helado	elado	ice cream
huevo	webo	egg
jugo	hoogo	fruit juice
langosta	langosta	lobster
leche	lecheh	milk
marisco	mareesko	seafood
mantequilla	mantekee-ya	butter
pan	pan	bread
papas	papas	potatoes
postre	postreh	dessert
pescado	peskado	fish
plátano	platano	banana
pollo	po-yo	chicken
potaje/sopa	potaheh/sopa	soup
puerco	pwairko	pork
queso	keso	cheese
refresco	refresko	drink
sal	sal	salt
salsa	salsa	sauce
té	teh	tea
vinagre	beenagreh	vinegar

Cuban Terms

apagón	apagon	black-out, power outage
babalawo	babala-wo	a priest of Afro-Cuban religion
batey	batay	village around sugar factory
carro	karro	car
casa de la trova	kasa deh la troba	club where traditional music is played
cayo	ka-yo	small island
chama	chama	child
criollo	kr-yo-yo	Creole (born in Cuba of Spanish descent)
divisas	deebeesas	dollars (slang)
eva	eba	woman
guagua	gwagwa	bus
guajiro	gwaheero	farmer
guarapo	gwarapo	sugar cane juice
ingenio	eenhen-yo	sugar factory complex
jama	hama	food, meal
jinetera	heenetaira	prostitute, or female hustler

jinetero	heenet**ai**ro	male person hustling tourists
libreta	leeb**re**ta	rations book
moneda	mo**ne**da	pesos ("national
nacional	nas-**yo**nal	currency")
moros y	**mo**ros ee	rice and black
cristianos	krist-**ya**nos	beans
paladar	palad**ar**	privately-owned restaurant
puro	**poo**ro	authentic Cuban cigar
santero	sant**ai**ro	santería priest
tabaco	tab**a**ko	low-quality cigar
tienda	t-**yen**da	shop that only accepts dollars
trago	**tra**go	alcoholic drink
tunas	**too**nas	prickly pears
zafra	s**a**fra	sugar cane harvest

Health

I don't feel well	**Me siento mal**	meh s-**yen**to mal
I have a...	**Me duele...**	meh dwel**e**...
stomach ache	**el estómago**	el est**o**mago
headache	**la cabeza**	la kab**e**sa
He/she is ill	**Está enfermo/a**	esta enf**ai**rmo
I need to rest	**Necesito**	neses**ee**to
	decansar	dek**a**nsar
drug store	**farmacia**	farmas**ee**-ya

Post Office and Bank

bank	**banco**	b**a**nko
I want to send	**Quiero enviar**	k-y**ai**ro emb-yar
a letter	**una carta**	**oo**na k**a**rta
postcard	**postal tarjeta**	postal t**a**rheta
stamp	**sello**	s**e**-yo
draw out money	**sacar dinero**	sakar deen**ai**ro

Shopping

How much is it?	**¿Cuánto cuesta?**	kw**a**nto kw**e**sta
What time do	**¿A qué hora**	a ke **o**ra abr**e**h/
you open/close?	**abre/ cierra?**	s-y**ai**rra
May I pay with a	**¿Puedo pagar**	pw**e**do pagar
credit card?	**con tarjeta**	kon t**a**rheta
	de crédito?	deh kr**e**deeto?

Sightseeing

beach	**playa**	pl**a**-ya
castle, fortress	**castillo**	kast**ee**-yo
cathedral	**catedral**	kated**ra**l
church	**iglesia**	eegl**e**s-ya
district	**barrio**	b**a**rr-yo
garden	**jardín**	hard**ee**n
guide	**guía**	g**ee**-a
house	**casa**	k**a**sa
motorway	**autopista**	owtop**ee**sta
museum	**museo**	moos**e**h-o
park	**parque**	p**a**rkeh
road	**carretera**	karret**ai**ra
square, plaza	**plaza, parque**	pl**a**sa, p**a**rkeh
street	**calle, callejón**	k**a**-ye, ka-yeh**o**n

town hall	**Ayuntamiento**	a-yoontam-y**en**to
tourist bureau	**buró de**	boor**o** deh
	turismo	toor**ee**smo

Numbers

0	**cero**	s**ai**ro
1	**uno**	**oo**no
2	**dos**	dos
3	**tres**	tres
4	**cuatro**	ku**a**tro
5	**cinco**	s**ee**nko
6	**seis**	s**a**ys
7	**siete**	s-y**e**teh
8	**ocho**	**o**cho
9	**nueve**	nw**e**beh
10	**diez**	d-yes
11	**once**	**o**nseh
12	**doce**	d**o**seh
13	**trece**	tr**e**seh
14	**catorce**	kat**o**rseh
15	**quince**	k**ee**nseh
16	**dieciséis**	d-yesees**a**ys
17	**diecisiete**	d-yesees-y**e**teh
18	**dieciocho**	d-yes-y**o**cho
19	**diecinueve**	d-yeseenw**e**beh
20	**veinte**	b**a**ynteh
30	**treinta**	tr**a**ynta
40	**cuarenta**	kw**a**renta
50	**cincuenta**	seenkw**e**nta
60	**sesenta**	ses**e**nta
70	**setenta**	set**e**nta
80	**ochenta**	och**e**nta
90	**noventa**	nob**e**nta
100	**cien**	s-yen

Time

minute	**minuto**	meen**oo**to
hour	**hora**	**o**ra
half-hour	**media hora**	med-ya **o**ra
Monday	**lunes**	l**oo**nes
Tuesday	**martes**	m**a**rtes
Wednesday	**miércoles**	m-y**ai**rkoles
Thursday	**jueves**	hw**e**bes
Friday	**viernes**	b-y**a**irnes
Saturday	**sábado**	s**a**bado
Sunday	**domingo**	dom**ee**ngo
January	**enero**	en**ai**ro
February	**febrero**	febr**ai**ro
March	**marzo**	m**a**rso
April	**abril**	abr**ee**l
May	**mayo**	m**a**-yo
June	**junio**	h**oo**n-yo
July	**julio**	h**oo**l-yo
August	**agosto**	ag**o**sto
September	**setiembre**	set-y**e**mbreh
October	**octubre**	okt**oo**breh
November	**noviembre**	nob-y**e**mbreh
December	**diciembre**	dees-y**e**mbreh